Hispaniola

✳✳✳✳✳✳

Hispaniola

Caribbean Chiefdoms in the Age of Columbus

Samuel M. Wilson

The University of Alabama Press
Tuscaloosa and London

Library of Congress Cataloging-in-Publication Data

Wilson, Samuel M.
Hispaniola : Caribbean chiefdoms in the age of Columbus / by Samuel M. Wilson.
p. cm.
Bibliography: p.
Includes index.
ISBN 0-8173-0462-2 (alk. paper)
1. Taino Indians—First contact with Occidental civilization.
2. Taino Indians—Kings and rulers.   3. Taino Indians—History.
4. Indians of the West Indies—Hispaniola—First contact with Occidental civilization.
5. Indians of the West Indies—Hispaniola—Kings and rulers.   6. Indians of the West
Indies—Hispaniola—History.   I. Title.
F1619.2.T3W55   1990
972.93'01—dc20
89-4907
CIP

British Library Cataloguing-in-Publication Data available

✳✳✳✳✳✳

Contents

✳✳✳✳✳✳

Illustrations

******

Preface

Five hundred years ago, the island of Hispaniola was the setting for one of the most dramatic encounters in human history. After tens of millennia of virtually total separation, the peoples of the New World and Old World began the process of mutual rediscovery. In the Caribbean, the newly expansionist European nation-states encountered the Indians of the New World. The encounter was cataclysmic for the indigenous peoples of the Caribbean, and for those of the island of Hispaniola especially. Ten years after Columbus's arrival all of the indigenous political institutions on Hispaniola had collapsed: twenty-five years after contact more than 90 percent of the population had died.

I undertook this study in part because I was interested in the ways in which complex societies emerged and flourished in human history. I was interested in the appearance and operation of enduring systems of social stratification, and especially in the appearance of political entities in which many villages allied under one leader. Many areas have seen such social and political developments, in many different periods: in Mesopotamia it occurred more than five millennia B.C.; in China complex societies emerged more than 2000 years B.C.; similar developments occurred in Olmec Mesoamerica a millennium later. The complex chiefdoms of the Caribbean emerged in the last few centuries before European contact—between A.D. 800 and 1492.

What circumstances surrounded the emergence of complex societies in the Caribbean? Archaeological data tell us of the migrations of people, the changes in pottery manufacture, artifact typology, settlement patterns, and population growth in the millennia preceding the Europeans arrival. Linguistic evidence allows us tentatively to reconstruct the relationship between the people of the Greater Antilles, the Lesser Antilles, and the South American mainland, and it offers historic scenarios for the length of time between the separations of the groups. Ethnohistorical and ethnographic data gathered among the peoples of mainland South and Central America who survived the traumatic arrival of the Europeans provide us with an image of what life may have been like for the Caribbean Indians and help us to understand how they viewed their world.

Finally, we have the eyewitness accounts of the Europeans who came to the New World first. Columbus and his party arrived late in the year 1492 on their way to Japan. For Columbus, his codiscoverers, and his royal and commercial backers, the Caribbean archipelago possessed tremendous economic potential. Gold was to be found there, especially on the island of Hispaniola. This book's narrative descriptions of the events of the contact period on Hispaniola are drawn primarily from these eyewitness accounts.

This book represents only a piece of the puzzle in trying to understand the development of the Caribbean chiefdoms. The documents from the contact period cover such a brief period, and a period of such cataclysmic change for the Indians of Hispaniola, that one cannot confidently extrapolate from the ethnohistorical present to the archaeological past. Strengthening the interconnections between archaeological and ethnohistorical data and research strategies remains a priority for the future in the Caribbean and elsewhere.

The story of Columbus's discoveries in the Caribbean—and indeed a great deal of the story of the contact period between the New World and the Old—is shadowed by tragedy and intense human suffering. The extraordinary events of the contact period, which played such a fundamental role in creating the modern world, were apocalyptic for many New World cultures, including the Taíno of the Greater Antilles. It is easy to encapsulate the catastrophe that occurred on Hispaniola in a remote historical era, one with little relevance for the modern world. From an archaeologist's perspective, however, five hundred years is a relatively short span of time: we are still in the "contact period" between the Old World and the New, between Western and non-Western peoples. The lessons of the encounter on Hispaniola are compelling today.

This project has been supported by many institutions, colleagues, and friends. I would like to acknowledge the help of several individuals and groups.

Irving Rouse, Robert McCormick Adams, Don Rice, Richard Klein, Karl Butzer, and Marshall Sahlins were my teachers and played a large part in deciding the directions this research would take. Research for this book was supported by the Tinker Foundation and the Mellon Foundation.

Several Caribbean scholars and institutions helped make the research possible. I especially thank Ricardo Alegría and his colleagues at the Centro de Estudios Avanzados Puertorriqueño y el Caribe and Elpidio Ortega and the staff of the Museo del Hombre Dominicano. In the Dominican Republic, I also thank Frank Moya Pons, Fabio de Jesus Pimentel and D. Manuel García Arévalo. On Puerto Rico, I would like to thank Diana Lopez and Miguel Rodriguez. Timothy Kane helped with the preparation of the manuscript, and Craig Noll provided expert editorial assistance. William F. Keegan's careful reading of the manuscript is gratefully acknowledged, and Irving Rouse's help has been immeasurable, both in the research and writing of this book and in my Caribbean studies generally. Any errors in fact or in interpretation, however, are mine alone.

Cory Wolf has helped in this project in too many ways to count, and I would like to acknowledge her comprehensive contribution. Finally, the book is dedicated to my parents, McCormick and Lorna Wilson, and my parents-in-law, William and Cornelia Wolf; they know that the book would never have been begun without their help.

✳✳✳✳✳✳

Hispaniola

1

******

Introduction

In the autumn of 1492 a Genoese merchant captain and ninety sailors attempted to find a more profitable route to Japan by sailing west across the Atlantic. The expedition was financed by the royal courts of Castille and Aragon, and to a large extent by the participants in the voyage. They all hoped to amass the kinds of personal and national fortunes that Portuguese traders had found on the west coast of Africa in the decades before. There was no question about falling off the edge of the earth: educated Europeans had known for centuries that the world was spherical. There was, however, considerable disagreement about how far it was from Spain to Japan. Even the highest estimates were less than half of the actual distance.

Three small ships sailed from Spain to the Canary Islands, and from there they were carried west by the trade winds and the north equatorial current of the Atlantic. They sailed out of sight of land for about a month. Instead of the marvelous eastern kingdoms described by Marco Polo and other European travelers, they found a vast archipelago of tropical islands that stretched 2,700 km (1,700 mi) from end to end. The islands were inhabited by people who were alien to them in appearance, customs, and language.

These "Indians" (the name itself connotes their misidentification) were the descendants of mainland South American people who had migrated into the Caribbean in the last centuries B.C. In fifteen hundred years they had colonized nearly all of the archipelago from Trinidad to the northern Bahamas. Their migration into the Caribbean had not been gradual but instead had proceeded as a series of rapid leaps followed by consolidation of the

1

occupied territory. In the process they replaced or incorporated smaller groups of inhabitants who had lived in the islands for several thousand years B.C.

In the five hundred years before the European explorers' arrival, elaborate and complex social and political institutions had developed in the Caribbean societies, especially in Puerto Rico and Hispaniola (the island containing the modern countries Dominican Republic and Haiti; see figure 1). The sociopolitical organization of these islands was similar in structure to mainland South American sociopolitical systems, with whom they shared an ancestry, and yet in a great many ways it was unique to the Caribbean. From archaeological evidence it is apparent that the complex sociopolitical institutions emerged in place in the islands, rather than being transported from the mainland. These people called themselves *Taíno*, from a root word meaning "noble" or "prudent" (Arrom 1975).

The Taíno Indians were the first group the Europeans encountered in their exploration of the New World. Hispaniola was the first foothold for the Spanish colonization and remained the most important base of operations in the New World for thirty years. The Indians of Hispaniola were thus the first in the New World to experience the avarice of the Europeans, their violent character and overwhelming military superiority, and the devastating assortment of diseases they carried. The Taíno were the first New World population to be quickly and completely eradicated as a consequence of the European discovery.

This book examines the contact period on Hispaniola, the short span of years between the first encounters with the Europeans in 1492 and the collapse of the indigenous chiefdoms. The data used are predominately historical and ethnohistorical; they are taken from the letters, accounts, journals, court cases, and histories of the conquest of the Caribbean islands by the Spanish in the fifteenth and sixteenth centuries. The explorers were very interested in the alien Taíno culture in the early years of the contact period and described their interactions with them in some detail. The Spanish were dependent on the good will of the Taíno *caciques* (the Taíno word for "chiefs" or "headmen") for their food and thus had to find a way to fit into the indigenous social and political spectra. This necessity occupied a great deal of their attention in the first few years of the contact period—until supply lines were firmly established from Spain and the local sociopolitical systems had collapsed.

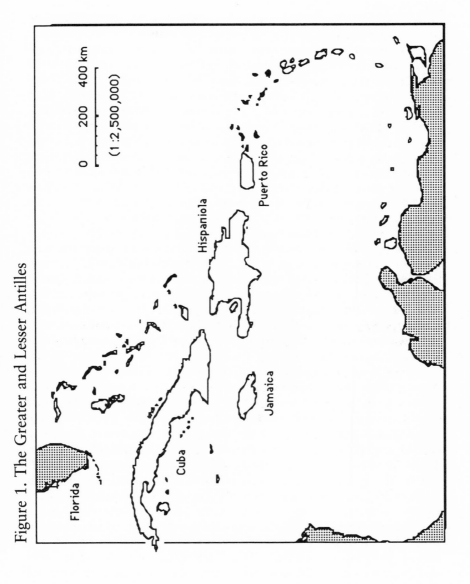

Figure 1. The Greater and Lesser Antilles

The Caribbean situation is nearly unique in the history of the contact period in the New World. After the Europeans' arrival in the Caribbean, stories of their strange appearance and practices spread rapidly. The European items the explorers brought for trade entered into the existing trade networks of elite goods and often preceded the explorers' arrival in a new area. Similarly, diseases were transmitted along the same trade and communication routes and often registered a demographic effect before the Europeans were there to see it happen. On Hispaniola, however, the process of mutual discovery began unannounced.

The sociopolitical organization of the Taíno Indians is also of special interest to anthropologists interested in how complex societies and governments came into being. The Taíno were organized politically into collective polities of dozens of villages, with one chief, or cacique, having paramount importance. The title of the cacique was inherited and carried special privileges and powers. He played a part in directing the production and distribution of food and goods of his chiefdom, or *cacicazgo*, and had a central role in mediating between the spiritual and physical world. He was the highest-ranking member of an elite stratum of society that was (to varying extents) separate from a nonelite or commoner stratum (Alcina Franch 1983; Dreyfus 1981; Moscoso 1978; Sanoja Obediente 1983; Sauer 1966; Vega 1980; Veloz Maggiolo 1972, 1977, 1983).

These characteristics make the Taíno sociopolitical system comparable to a wide range of chiefdom societies that have existed worldwide in the last several millennia. The variability of these chiefdom societies, and their place in the trajectory of historical processes that led to more complex empires and states, has been extensively debated in the anthropological literature (Carneiro 1970, 1983; Creamer and Haas 1985; Drennan and Uribe 1987; Earle 1977, 1987; Feinman and Neitzel 1984; Fried 1967; Friedman 1974; Haas 1982; Kirch 1984; Service 1971; Spencer 1987; Upham 1987).

In this book I reconstruct in narrative fashion a series of events from the early contact period and place the events, the actors, and their motivations in as rich and complete a historical context as possible. This reconstructed context draws on the product of centuries of historical, archaeological, and cultural anthropological scholarship concerning the early voyages of discovery, the explorers themselves, and the New World peoples they encountered.

Particular attention is paid in the narratives to the interactions of the elite stratum of Taíno society—its patterns of succession, inheritance, marriage, trade, and warfare—and the processes through which these multivillage polities were held together as a unified entity.

Using historical data from the sources available from the early contact period has many inherent problems. Observations of the Spanish and Italian chroniclers of the period were conditioned by their own theories or prevailing European interpretations. Taíno culture was viewed through fifteenth-century European eyes, and the written records that survived were often crafted with particular political objectives in mind. The journal that Cristóbal Colón[1] kept on the first voyage, for example, was above all his report to the king and queen and was designed to show him and his decisions in the best possible light. The Dominican friar Bartolomé de las Casas wrote his extensive works to chronicle what he perceived to be the brutal destruction of the Indian populations at the hands of the Spanish. Others (e.g. Gonzalo Fernández de Oviedo y Valdés) took the perspective that the Indians were little more than a curious feature of the natural environment.

Nondocumentary sources of information have also proved useful in the present study. Archaeological data from the Greater and Lesser Antilles (discussed below) help in the reconstruction and description of Taíno culture, and in some cases historical descriptions of villages visited by the Spaniards can be correlated with their archaeological remains (e.g. Deagan 1985; Goodwin and Walker 1975; Veloz Maggiolo et al. 1976). In a more general sense, artifacts and physical or architectural remains can be associated with ethnohistorical descriptions of their use and meaning.

Modern geographical tools as simple as a detailed map provide an interpretive advantage that the explorers did not have. Another dimension is added to the ethnohistorical and archaeological record by more recent ethnographic work among South American

---

[1] This was the name by which the explorer was known in his business dealings in Andalusia (Giménez Fernández 1951; Perez de Tudela 1983; Pike 1966, 1972; Remeu de Armas 1985) and by which he was referenced in his own writings and other documents from the period (Las Casas; Columbus 1893). In Genoa his family name was Colombo. In French he is Christophe Colomb; in English, Christopher Columbus.

Indian groups that are linguistically and historically related to the Taíno (Alegría 1978; Arrom 1967; Sanoja Obediente 1983; Siegel 1988).

Any reconstruction of the events of the early contact period, and of Taíno culture generally, must incorporate these diverse sources of data and make effective use of them. Each set of data, however, lies in the domain of different traditional disciplines—history, anthropology, archaeology, and human geography. In a period in which disciplinary boundaries are frequently and easily crossed, the problem remains to find a methodology and mode of explanation that is equal to its integrative task (Campbell 1969). The use of narrative, traditionally a tool of the historian, has reemerged as a vehicle for relating causal explanation (Stone 1979). This trend may reflect a growing consensus about the complexity of human societies and the inability of past (and current) normative approaches to explain this complexity adequately (Hodder 1987a, 1987b).

The approach taken in this study combines historical description in a narrative form with anthropological interpretation. This method derives in part from anthropological interpretations of historical and ethnohistorical data such as Sahlins's in Polynesia (1981, 1985) and Geertz's in Indonesia (1980), as well as a historical tradition of applying anthropological models and interpretations to documentary evidence (as in Braudel's *Civilization and Capitalism*, 1981–84) within a broadly historical rubric (Braudel 1980, LeRoy Ladurie 1981). Geertz's concept of anthropological analysis as "thick description" (1973:3–30) is an important point of departure for the present study.

A narrative style is appealing in dealing with the ethnohistorical documents of the conquest period in the Caribbean in part because of the analytical limitations the documents possess. Only in a very limited way could they be reified to a quantifiable set of data acceptable to the more numerically oriented schools of historiography or anthropology. Associated with every piece of ethnohistoric information is a sort of confidence value; not every observation or opinion can be afforded the same certainty. The narrative method thus offers a forum in which different classes and qualities of data can be presented in a similar context.

Another reason for approaching the historical documents in a narrative fashion is to attempt to tackle in a new way a problem encountered by earlier analyses of the Taíno. Many of the ethnohistorical studies undertaken on the Taíno in this century have organized documentary material via a normative methodology (similar to the editorial structure of Julian Steward's *Handbook of South American Indians*), examining Taíno cultural traits as they fall into a series of categories (Cassá 1974; Gómez Acevedo and Ballesteros Gaibrois 1980; Rouse 1948; Sauer 1966; Tabío and Rey 1966; Veloz Maggiolo 1972). This strategy also appears in earlier interpretations of the Indians of the Caribbean (Charlevoix 1731–33; Nau 1894). This categorical or trait-list approach has been very productive, imposing an interpretive structure on the diverse documents from the contact period. Within this framework, however, it is difficult to avoid presenting Taíno sociopolitical institutions as relatively static and discrete entities. The view emphasized here is of a sociopolitical system that was highly integrated. That is, it is almost impossible (and perhaps counterproductive) to separate the social and symbolic roles of a Taíno cacique from his political roles, or to differentiate the economic from the ceremonial importance of Taíno feasts (Helms 1980, 1988; Sahlins 1981).

Concerning the Ethnohistorical Sources

The documents used in this study are taken both as compilations of historical data with varying degrees of accuracy and as texts within a European literary context. Because of the richness and vitality of the documents, and because they recount stories which are our principal concern in this book, it is easy to lose sight of the intellectual and literary milieus to which the documents contributed and within which they must be assessed.

The sixteenth century was a crucial turning point in the intellectual history of Europe. The discovery of the New World coincided with the full florescence of the Italian Renaissance and just preceded the emergence of Renaissance thought in northern Europe and England. Leonardo da Vinci (1452–1519) and Michelangelo (1475–1564) were contemporaries of the events examined in this study. Through the literary genius of writers like Shakespeare (1564–1616), the cultural structures of the Middle Ages were transformed and given a modern, secular voice. Patterns of rational or scientific inquiry which persist to the present were novel and audacious at the time. Copernicus's *Concerning the Revolutions of Celestial Orbs* appeared in 1543, as did Vesalius's *Concerning the Structure of the Human*

Body, and both met with tremendous popular and ecclesiastical criticism.

The ways in which information was disseminated were also changing radically just as Las Casas, Martyr, and Oviedo were writing. The diffusion from China of practical kinds of paper and the invention of a printing device with movable type (the first Gutenberg Bible was printed around 1454) provided the functional basis for scholarship to become a secular enterprise. It is estimated that by the year 1500 more than twenty-five thousand separate editions of books had been produced, totaling perhaps as many as twenty million volumes (Febvre and Martin 1971:368). Between 1480 and 1500 the first printing shops had opened in Spain (p. 262).

The degree to which the chroniclers of the conquest of the Caribbean were participants in the European intellectual revolutions differs in each case. On one hand, Pietro Martyr d'Anghiera, an Italian intellectual, was the archetypal Renaissance thinker. He was brought to the court of Castille to tutor the royal heirs precisely because he represented the Renaissance intellectual tradition of Dante, Petrarch, and Boccaccio. On the other hand, Cristóbal Colón has been aptly described by Todorov as a "medieval mentality" whose spiritual worldview stands in such sharp contrast to the emerging secular vision of the Renaissance (1984:1–13). According to Todorov, Colón's passion for discovery was motivated by his dream of providing money for the liberation of Jerusalem from the infidels (p. 10)—a rebirth of Crusader ideals three hundred years out of date.

The most important series of documents used in this study are the writings of Fray Bartolomé de Las Casas. In practical ways Las Casas embodied the humanistic concerns of the Renaissance, while embracing the philosophy of the older sacred order. He was born in Seville in 1474 and was educated at the University at Salamanca (Giménez Fernández 1971). His father, a merchant, and uncle had gone to the New World on one of the early voyages, perhaps the second or third voyage of Colón. In 1502, when he was around twenty-eight, Las Casas followed them to the New World. He became a priest on Hispaniola but participated in the brutal conquest of Cuba. There he was a landholder and *encomendero* with Indian slaves. His strong and unpopular convictions about the treatment of the Indians did not manifest themselves until a dramatic conversion experience in 1514. He participated in an unsuccessful attempt to colonize Venezuela, lived for periods in the Valley of Mexico and in Guatemala, and was made bishop of Chiapas. Returning to Spain in 1547 at the age of seventy-three, he continued work on his major manuscripts. He lived to be ninety-two years old, dying in 1566 (Hanke 1970:i–xviii).

The written work for which Las Casas is most famous is the *Brevísima relación de la destrucción de las Indias*. This short tract damned the Spanish treatment of the Indians of the New World, recounting atrocities committed by the conquistadores and documenting the scope of the genocide that had taken place. The *Brevísima relación* was probably written in Spain after his return from Mexico in 1547 and was published in Seville in 1552. It was Las Casas's only major work to be published during his lifetime. Quickly translated and republished throughout Europe, this polemic propagated the "Black Legend" of the Spanish conquest (Las Casas 1966).

His two multivolume histories, *Historia de las Indias* and *Apologética historia sumaria*, combine recursive philosophical deliberations about the great classical texts (in the Renaissance style of the day) with extremely careful and encyclopedic narrations of the events of the conquest period. His narrative proceeds methodically in the third person, with sentences sometimes running to one thousand words. He reproduces, sometimes imaginatively, dialogues and long speeches in the course of the 267-chapter *Apologética* and the 300-chapter *Historia*. His narration is punctuated by passionate or despondent reflections; most of the Indians that he had tried to protect (including almost all of those on Hispaniola) had died.

The *Historia* was probably begun in 1527, when Las Casas was living at the Dominican monastery at Puerto Plata, on the north coast of Hispaniola. Samuel Eliot Morison, one of Colón's most perceptive biographers, calls the *Historia* "the one book on the discovery of America that I should wish to preserve if all others were destroyed" (1942:51). The *Apologética* may also have been started in 1527, or perhaps at that point they were the same manuscript (Hanke 1970). Las Casas began these monumental projects in response to the publication in 1526 of *Historia general de las Indias*, by Gonzalo Fernández de Oviedo y Valdés. Oviedo had arrived on Hispaniola around 1512 after most of the Taíno were dead (Cook and Borah 1971; Rosenblat 1967), and his *Historia general* (as well as his *Sumario de la natural historia de las Indias*) was largely concerned with the flora, fauna, and geography of the islands. Las Casas felt that Oviedo, not having experienced the destruction of the Indian population, or perhaps merely insensitive to it, had viewed the Indians as simply another interesting peculiarity of the Indies (cf. Friede 1971).

Las Casas's histories were not published when they were finished. For all of their importance for the study of the New World, they were published hundreds of years later—*Historia de las Indias* in 1875 (Madrid: Fondo de Cultura Económica) and *Apologética historia sumaria* in 1909 (Madrid: Nueva Biblioteca de Autores Españoles). It is likely that the *Historia de las Indias* was finished first, possibly in the twenty years between 1527 and Las Casas's return to Spain in 1547. The more introspective *Apologética* seems to have been revised and rewritten in Las Casas's old age (O'Gorman 1967:xv–lxxix).

We may chafe at the limitations inherent in the documents from the conquest period, but without the insight and sensitivity of Las Casas, his vision and narrative voice, we would have just a fraction of the information that exists about the Taíno Indians. We are doubly fortunate, however, in that there was another equally extraordinary observer on the scene—Pietro Martyr d'Anghiera.

Martyr was perhaps the first person in Europe to realize the importance of Colón's discovery. He quickly undertook to spread the news of the discovery within the stratum of the European intellegentsia, and his careful accounts of the events were the first to leave Spain. Having access to the correspondence of Ferdinand and Isabela, and thus to Colón's "Memorandum" and "Journal" of the first voyage, he began to send letters in Latin to Italy as soon as Colón had returned from the Caribbean. He also interviewed many of the participants of the voyages, including Colón, and in some respects, was in a better position than anyone to take a synthetic view of the New World. There was a great demand for Martyr's accounts, and letters from his correspondents and others (including Pope Alexander VI) urgently demanded more. The first compilations of these writings were published in Italian in 1504 and 1507, and editions including the latest letters were issued throughout the sixteenth century (MacNutt 1970:1–54). MacNutt's English translation from the Latin, used in this study, was taken from nine Latin editions which appeared in the sixteenth century (pp. 49–54).

Pietro Martyr was a foreigner who was highly favored in the court of Ferdinand and Isabela, arguably the most powerful monarchs in Europe. His accounts, not surprisingly, take a view of events that is favorable to the king and queen. Nevertheless, even when Colón was under arrest in Spain, Martyr did not detract from the significance of his accomplishments. His biases are strongest in considering the actions of rival Spanish factions on Hispaniola. Between his narratives, those of Las Casas (who was also a supporter of the Colón family), and the writings of Colón himself, we are left with a one-sided view of the revolts of Roldán and others (see chapter 3 and Ramos Peréz 1982). For all three writers, whose works provide the majority of material used in this study, their biases concerning the Indians were brought about principally by their inabilities to understand what they were seeing, rather than by an intent to mislead the reader. Even for Las Casas, the "protector of the Indians," it is subjectively clear where his description stops and his polemic begins.

Cristóbal Colón was his own publicist; his most important writings were intended for Ferdinand and Isabela. Two documents from the first voyage are particularly valuable, for apart from Martyr's synthetic accounts, there are almost no other records of the voyage. The first is known as the "Journal," a document of about fifty thousand words, which describes the day-to-day events of provisioning the ship, the first crossing, arriving in the Bahamas, sailing to Cuba and then to Hispaniola, the wreck of the *Santa María*, the construction of Navidad, and the return to Spain. The location of the original journal, if it still exists, is unknown. It was in possession of the court for some time after its writing, however, because Martyr had seen it, and Las Casas had had the opportunity to make a partial copy of it. Colón's son Fernando, in his *Historia del Almirante de las Indias, Don Cristóbal Colón* (1824), also includes a partial copy. Navarrete's *Colección de los viages y descubrimientos que hicieron por mar los Españoles desde fines del siglo XV* (1825–37) contains Las Casas's hand-copied version, as does Kerr's edition (1824).

The second important document from the first voyage is Colón's précis of his journal, which he wrote on the return trip. Although intended for the king and queen, it is known as the "letter to Santangel" or the "letter to Raphael Sánchez." It was somewhat more carefully worded and self-serving than the journal (the sinking of the *Santa María* was not mentioned) and was widely copied and distributed. The letter appears in many collections, including Navarrete (1825) and Major (1924).

Of the writings of Colón, or the Admiral, these two documents are the most valuable for an analysis of the Indians of the Caribbean. Colón's many letters from later voyages and those written in Spain chart the progressive decline of his health, of his ability to govern the colonies, and of his royal favor.

There are two other letters from the second voyage which are significant for this study. The physician Diego Alvarez Chanca wrote the most detailed account which goes beyond Colón's letter to the crown about the first part of the second voyage (the "Torres Memorandum" or "Memorial de Colón para los Reyes-Católicos," in Navarrete 1825, vol. I). The Chanca letter appears in Major's edition of 1847. Chanca describes finding the destruction of Navidad, the founding of Isabela, and the marches inland to the goldfields. The letter by Michele de Cuneo, another Genoese, describes the same events in a more abbreviated form. This document appears in the Italian collection celebrating the four-hundred-year anniversary of the discovery (*Raccolta di documenti e studi,* 1893).

Another document providing tangential information concerning Taíno social and political organization is the *Interrogatorio jeronimiano* of 1517 (Archivo General de Indias, Sevilla, Sección Indiferente, legajo 1624). The interrogatorio contains testimony that was collected concerning the character and treatment of the Indians. The indigenous population was extremely reduced by that time, and the document describes a significantly transformed system, although terms implying sociopolitical status such as *cacique* and *nitaíno* are used (Rodríguez Demorizi 1971).

Colón assigned a Jeronymite friar named Ramón Pané to live among two groups of Indians on Hispaniola. As will be discussed in chapter 3, he lived with the Macorix people of the Vega Real, and then in the village of the cacique Guarionex. He produced a short description of his observations which contains a brief discussion of Taíno cosmology, listing five principal gods and including a partial origins myth. The original is lost, but Martyr and Las Casas had made notes on the document, which have survived. Much of the work is copied in Martyr's *De Orbe Novo.* A version in Italian appeared in 1571 which seems to have come from a nearly complete original. The versions used in this paper are the English (Bourne 1906) and Spanish (Pané 1974) translations from the Italian document, with comments taken from the notes of Martyr and Las Casas.

About the Translations

All of the passages from Las Casas's *Historia de las Indias, Apologética historia sumaria,* and *Brevísima relación de la destrucción de las Indias* are original translations from Spanish made for this study, as are the passages taken from Oviedo's *Historia general de las Indias* and *Sumario de la natural historia de las Indias*. Quotations taken from the Chanca and Coma letters are also translated from Navarrete's Spanish editions, and passages of the Cuneo letter are translations of the Italian version in *Raccolta di documenti e studi*. Part of Fernando Colón's biography of his father is taken from Kerr's 1824 translation, and part (reflected in the citations) is a new translation from Navarrete's compilation. MacNutt's 1912 English translation (reprinted in 1970) of the Latin text of Peter Martyr D'Anghiera's *De Orbe Novo* has been used. Passages from Girolamo Benzioni's late and derivative *History of the New World* have been taken from the Hakluyt translation from the Italian.

For the sake of continuity, all of the quotations from the work of recent scholars have also been presented in English translations.

Organization of the Book

The three narratives related in this book cover parts of the first eight years of the Spanish occupation of Hispaniola, from late 1492 until 1500. Each deals with events which elucidate aspects of the Taíno's culture and sociopolitical order.

Chapter 2 relates the events of the first voyage—the events in Europe that preceded the trip, the landing in the Bahamas, the voyage through the Bahamas and along northern Cuba, and the discovery of Hispaniola. Colón and his exploring party reached the northwest coast of Hispaniola in December 1492, after making landfall in the Bahamas and sailing along the northeast coast of Cuba. On Christmas eve, while most of the *Santa María*'s hands were asleep, an inexperienced pilot grounded the ship on a shoal. A cacique named Guacanagarí, whose village was close by, helped in salvaging the wreck. Because the remaining caravel, the *Niña* (the *Pinta* had gone off on its own and did not rejoin Colón's group until early January), could not accommodate all of the Spaniards, and because of the hospitality of Guacanagarí, Colón had a small blockhouse built and called it Navidad. He left thirty-eight men at Navidad and, on January 4, 1493, sailed eastward.

The narrative dealing with the first voyage of discovery covers several topics. It recounts the first meeting between the Europeans and the Caribbean islanders, when each group tried to make sense of the other in terms of the categories of their own culture. Here we may observe, especially in Colón's journal, the learning process on the part of the Europeans. In the first narrative Colón and his men visit the villages of some of the local rulers on northwest Hispaniola, and through their accounts we are introduced to the conventions of Taíno elite hospitality.

The second narrative begins with the events of the second voyage of Colón. When Colón arrived at Hispaniola, he found the colony of Navidad in ashes and all the men dead. After avoiding the Admiral as long as he could, Guacanagarí gave several confusing and contradictory accounts of the situation, settling finally on one that is recorded by Martyr.

> There are on the island, which is very large, a number of kings, who are more powerful than [Guacanagarí]; two of these, disturbed by the news of the arrival of the Spaniards, assembled considerable forces, attacked and killed our men and burned their entrenchments, houses and possessions; Guaccanarillo [Las Casas: Guacanagarí] had striven to save our men, and in the struggle had been wounded with an arrow. (1970:78)

Through this and other events and conversations, we are introduced to the political geography of the island, the size and distribution of the major chiefdoms, and the personalities of members of the Taíno elite. With little to be gained in pursuing Guacanagarí's role in the destruction of Navidad, Colón sent ships eastward to establish a new settlement. Isabela was established midway along the north coast of the island and was the principal Spanish port until the founding of Santo Domingo in early 1497.

There is considerable debate concerning the boundaries of the chiefdoms on Hispaniola and the identity of their principal caciques (Charlevoix 1731–33; Frati 1929; Loven 1935; Rouse 1948; Sauer 1966; Tolentino Rojas 1944; Vega 1980; Veloz Maggiolo 1972). Figure 2 is my reconstruction based on documents pertaining specifically to the years before 1500. Even during this short period, boundaries shifted between the cacicazgos, and a great deal of the island was probably not recognized as the province of any of the major caciques. Therefore, the central areas of cacicazgos are marked. It is possible that there were other equally important political units on the island at contact, possibly on the Samaná peninsula in the northeast and on the south coast, but they are not specified in the documents.

The second narrative (chapter 3) also discusses another individ-

Figure 2. Reconstructed cacicazgo centers in 1492

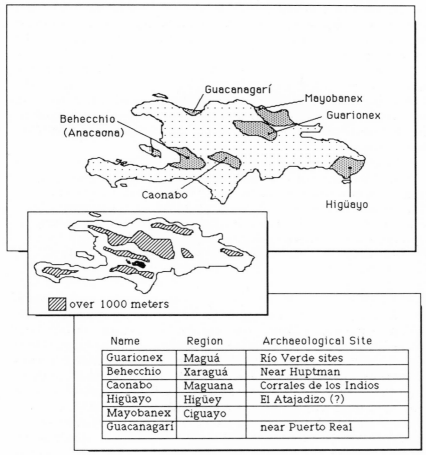

Name	Region	Archaeological Site
Guarionex	Maguá	Río Verde sites
Behecchio	Xaraguá	Near Huptman
Caonabo	Maguana	Corrales de los Indios
Higüayo	Higüey	El Atajadizo (?)
Mayobanex	Ciguayo	
Guacanagarí		near Puerto Real

ual who was central to the events of the conquest period—Guarionex, whose territory was centered in the large plain of the Vega Real. In order to make the goldfields secure for mining, Colón spent the years 1494 to 1498 building a series of small forts stretching from north to south across the island (Sauer 1966). Many of these small forts impinged on the territory under Guarionex's control, and relations between the Spaniards and Taíno became increasingly strained and violent. Between November 1494, when the first major battle in the Vega Real occurred, and July 1498, Guarionex tried to coordinate peaceful relations between the scattered and increasingly fractious Europeans and the desperate Indians of the Vega Real. By mid-1498 this had become impossible, and he escaped to the northern cordillera and the protection of an allied cacique named Mayobanex. Colón's brother Bartolomé—either pursuing a personal vendetta or believing that Guarionex still represented a threat—marched against Mayobanex's people in a three-month campaign to capture Guarionex. Through these events, which span the effective breakdown of indigenous sociopolitical structures in the Vega Real, we have a better representation of the nature of a cacique's power, his roles in Taíno society, and the limits to his authority.

The events in the third narrative (chapter 4) occurred in late 1496 or early 1497, when Bartolomé led a reconnaissance force to visit the province of Xaraguá in western Hispaniola. The Adelantado (Bartolomé Colón's title, given him by his brother) led a group of Spaniards from Santo Domingo to Xaraguá, to demand tribute from the Indians there. A cacique called Behecchio was the political ruler of this chiefdom, which was located on the Cul-de-Sac plain near modern Port-au-Prince, Haiti.

The Adelantado is a principal actor in many of the events related in this book. Colón himself was usually off on other voyages in the Caribbean, or in Spain trying to bolster his royal and commercial support. Until 1500, then, the Adelantado was the de facto leader of the Spanish forces loyal to the Colón family (Floyd 1973). Bartolomé was also a real partner in the Colón family's enterprises (Ballesteros y Beretta 1945; Pérez de Tudela 1954). Like his elder brother he possessed the gift of gracious audacity, even though he was the son of a Genoese weaver (Morison 1942; Perez de Tudela 1983). Unlike the Admiral, he had a gift for languages and some appreciation and understanding of Taíno culture; he was accustomed to the ways of the courts of kings, a skill which can be seen in the accounts of his visit to Xaraguá.

In the events that transpired during the trip to Xaraguá, we have the most substantial clues concerning the patterns of succession and inheritance among the Taíno elite. Particularly important are the suggestions of ways in which smaller chiefdoms coalesced into larger ones.

The remainder of this introductory chapter reviews the prehistory of the Caribbean, beginning with the first occupation of the islands by preceramic hunter-gatherers in the last 5,000 years B.C. The archaeological research on the Taíno that has been carried out on Hispaniola is then discussed, as is the ethnohistorical research on the Greater Antillean Taíno.

The Prehistoric Background of the Taíno Indians

The Taíno Indians of the Greater Antilles were the descendants of South American people who, over nearly five thousand years, had moved from the central Amazon to northeastern South America and into the Caribbean archipelago (Lathrap 1970; Roosevelt 1980; Rouse 1985; Rouse and Cruxent 1963). Reconstructing the movement of population groups involves the interplay of historical linguistic studies (Brochado 1984; Lemle 1971; Noble 1965; Rouse 1985; Taylor and Rouse 1955) and archaeological research in the Amazon Basin (Lathrap 1970; Meggers 1971; Meggers and Evans 1961), the Orinoco (Roosevelt 1980; Rouse and Allaire 1978; Rouse and Cruxent 1963), and the northeast coast of South America (Boomert 1983). While the correlation between linguistic and archaeological research is not perfect, and questions remain (particularly concerning the dating of developments which preceded the colonization of the Antilles [Roosevelt 1980; Rouse and Allaire 1978; Sanoja Obediente and Vargas 1983; Zucchi et al. 1984]), the broad outlines of a population movement from the Amazon through the Orinoco basin to the northeast coast seems most reasonable on present evidence (see Rouse n.d., 1985).

At the headwaters of the Orinoco and on the Guyanese coastal plain, the groups of people who were the antecedents of the Caribbean Indians lived in villages along relatively productive riverine terraces. Their tropical-forest horticultural economy was based on root crops, animal protein from the rivers and forests, and probably some maize agriculture (Boomert 1978, 1983; Keegan 1987; Roosevelt 1980; Rouse and Cruxent 1963; Versteeg 1980, but cf. Sanoja Obediente and Vargas 1983; Zucchi et al. 1984). When sedentary agricultural people moved into the Lesser Antilles from South America in the last centuries B.C., they brought this economic and settlement strategy with them.

When they moved into the Caribbean islands, some were already inhabited by a small population of nonagricultural people. The Caribbean archipelago appears to have been colonized first around 5000 B.C., when people moved into the islands of the Greater Antilles via the Lesser Antilles, or from Central America via the now-submerged mid-Caribbean islands that stretch between the eastern tip of Honduras and Nicaragua and the island of Jamaica (Keegan and Diamond 1987; Nicholson 1976c; Rouse and Allaire 1978:465; Veloz Maggiolo and Ortega 1973; Veloz Maggiolo and Vega 1982). Presently the later route seems more likely; no archaeological evidence of these early immigrants, whose lithic tool kit is called Casimiroid (Rouse 1986:130, fig. 23), has been found in the Lesser Antilles, and there are similarities between Central American and Casimiroid stone tools (Coe 1957; Callaghan 1985).

The second migration into the Caribbean occurred around 3000 B.C. and has clear artifactual antecedents on the South American mainland. Like the Casimiran migration, these people—whose aceramic artifact assemblage is called Ortoiroid—apparently did not practice horticulture. Their economy was principally oriented toward the collection of coastal and shallow-reef foods (Armstrong 1978; Davis 1982; Koslowski 1978; Lundberg 1980; Rouse 1986). Their small settlements are usually located in proximity to these resources. The occurrence of adzes made of conch flares (*Strombus gigas*), ethnohistorically seen to be used in canoe manufacture, and the diverse origins of the chert used in their stone tools, as well as the wide distribution of Ortoiroid sites in the Lesser Antilles, attest to their competence in ocean travel (Armstrong 1979; Keegan and Diamond 1987; Nicholson 1976c). It has been suggested that some (Nicholson 1983:6) or all (Keegan 1985:53; Keegan and Diamond 1987:64) of the Lesser Antilles were abandoned about 1000 years B.C., but the ^{14}C determination of 540 ±60 B.C. from a preceramic site on Nevis (Wilson 1989) indicates that this conclusion may be premature.

In the last few centuries B.C., sedentary horticultural people moved into the Caribbean from the northeast coast of South America. Their ceramics, including a distinctive decorative style of red and white painting, are of the Saladoid series.

The Saladoid frontier moved through the Lesser Antilles rapidly to Puerto Rico, the first of the Greater Antilles. The earliest radiocarbon dates for Saladoid material are presently from St. Martin, where the Hope Estate site has produced dates of 325 ±60 B.C. and 290 ±45 B.C. (based on charcoal; Haviser, personal communication, 1988). On Puerto Rico the earliest dates are 160 ±80 B.C. from El Convento, 110 ±70 from Hacienda Grande, and 110 ±60 from Maisabel (Rouse and Alegría 1989). With the exception of the eastern end of Hispaniola, Puerto Rico was the northwesternmost extension of this migration for the next five hundred years or more (Rouse and Alegría 1989).

Artifacts representing aspects of the symbolic system recorded by Spanish explorers among the contact period with Taíno Indians of the Greater Antilles (chapter 4) were present in the earliest

Saladoid settlements. One example is the presence of three-pointed carved figurines: similar *zemi* or *cemí* artifacts represented the spirit helpers or supernatural allies of the contact-period chiefs of the Greater Antilles (Arnáiz 1983; Arrom 1967, 1975; Chanlatte Baik 1985; Olsen 1974a; Sued Badillo 1978).

Through the first millennium A.D. the societies of the Lesser Antilles, descendants of the Saladoid colonizers, underwent changes that are not yet clearly understood. Food preferences as represented in archaeological faunal samples changed, arguably as a result of overexploitation or technological innovation (Goodwin 1979, 1980; Keegan 1988; Wing and Scudder 1980, 1983). Decorative and formal aspects of ceramic assemblages changed as well, although at different times on different islands (McKusick 1960; Clerc 1968; Hoffman 1963, 1979; Allaire 1973, Rouse 1976; Rouse and Allaire 1978). On the basis of present evidence, house construction changed (Versteeg 1987a, 1987b; Siegel 1988; Siegel and Bernstein 1987). Patterns of settlement locational preference appear to have changed as well (Bradstreet and Figueredo 1974; Bullen 1964; Goodwin 1979; Sleight 1962; Watters 1980). Population size clearly increased through the first millennium A.D., although the trajectory of that growth is still not clearly understood (Keegan 1985; Goodwin 1979; Wilson 1989).

The discontinuation of white-on-red painting, a diagnostic decorative attribute of Saladoid pottery, and the resumed use of modeled incision as a decorative technique mark the classificatory boundary between the Saladoid and the subsequent Ostionoid ceramic series (Rouse 1986:143–44; Rouse and Allaire 1978:464). This transition appears to have occurred around A.D. 600, although white-on-red painting continued longer on some islands (e.g. Antigua, Hoffman 1963, 1979; Rouse 1976; D. Davis, personal communication). Rouse sees the post-Saladoid ceramic development in the Leeward Islands as having affinities with contemporary developments in the Virgin Islands and eastern Puerto Rico and classifies the ceramics of all three areas in the Elenan subseries of the Ostionoid ceramic series (Rouse and Allaire 1978; Rouse 1986:143).

Concomitant with the appearance of Ostionoid series ceramics after A.D. 600, archaeological evidence for the colonization by sedentary agriculturists of the Greater Antilles beyond Puerto Rico, especially Hispaniola, increases markedly (Veloz Maggiolo 1972; Veloz Maggiolo, Ortega, and Caba Fuentes 1981). This perceived movement is viewed by Rouse as the continued advance of the Saladoid frontier: "The Ostionan Ostionoids recommenced the previous Cedrosan Saladoid movement, expanding westward at the expense of the Courian Casimiroid people of the Archaic Age" (1986:144). An alternative to Rouse's (1983, 1986) view of the punctuated advance of a sedentary agricultural "frontier" is that the perceived "colonization" of Hispaniola is the archaeological manifestation of a pattern of logistic growth of populations that immigrated to Hispaniola earlier (Keegan 1985). The paucity of regional settlement research on Hispaniola (Wilson 1986; cf. Bullen and Bullen 1979; Ortega 1978) and well-dated sites from the second half of the first millennium A.D. renders the question moot at present.

When European observers arrived in the southern islands of the Lesser Antilles (the Windward Islands), they were occupied by an ethnic group called the Island Caribs. Male Island Caribs maintained a cultural and linguistic affiliation with mainland Carib groups. Their "men's language," used in ritual and trade, was a vestige of this linguistic heritage (Taylor and Hoff 1980:312; Dreyfus-Gamelon 1976). The dominant "women's language" was an Arawakan language historically related to the Igneri language of the Saladoid people and to the Taíno language of the Greater Antilles (Rouse n.d.). The correspondence of Suazoid ceramics with the historical Island Caribs is far from perfect (cf. Allaire 1980, 1984; Davis n.d.; Goodwin 1979; Sued Badillo 1978), and the difficult problem of the archaeological correlates for the Island Caribs remains unresolved.

The florescence of complex sociopolitical institutions had already begun in the Greater Antilles by A.D. 1000. When Europeans arrived in 1492, they found complex chiefdoms of hundreds of allied villages (Alcina Franch 1983; Cassá 1974; Dreyfus 1981; Sauer 1966; Rouse 1948; Wilson 1985a, 1985b, 1986). These people were known to the European explorers collectively as the Taíno. The Ostionoid ceramic series had diverged into two subseries on Hispaniola—the Meillacan and the Chican—and apparently both subseries were in use at the time of European contact (Wilson 1986).

The Archaeology of the Taíno on Hispaniola

In its ability to provide concrete detail about Taíno society, the archaeological evidence is much less developed than the ethnohistorical. It is, however, the most promising area in which new information on the Taíno of Hispaniola may be gained. Particularly for issues concerning the origins and development of the Taíno chiefdoms, archaeological evidence will provide the primary data.

Early archaeological work on Hispaniola was done by Rouse at Fort Liberté (1939, 1941) and Krieger on the Samaná peninsula (1930, 1931), and continued with the work of Boyrie de Moya (1960), Herrera Fritot, and others in the 1940s through the 1960s.

In the 1970s a sustained program of archaeological research was undertaken by the archaeologists associated with the Museo del Hombre Dominicano, the Universidad Autónoma de Santo Domingo, and the Fundación García Arévalo. For ten years a cadre of archaeologists and specialists (including Caba Fuentes, García Arévalo, Luna Calderón, Ortega, Pina Peña, Rímoli, Tavares, Vega, and especially Veloz Maggiolo) conducted extensive archaeological research throughout the Dominican Republic. Their work was organized by general strategies for dealing with each time period from the preceramic to the historical period. The late prehistoric period was given the least attention, because this period had the best alternative source of information in the ethnohistorical documents. An exception was the museo's research at El Atajadizo, a large ceremonial center (Veloz Maggiolo et al. 1976).

To provide a framework of archaeological correlates for the ethnohistorical study presented in this paper, five dimensions of the archaeological data are particularly important. They include the settlement patterns of the Taíno, the evidence for trade in prestige goods, the information obtained from burials, the suggestions of extra-Caribbean contacts or "diffusion," and the ongoing effort at constructing accurate chronological sequences for the island. These five issues are not uniformly well addressed in the archaeological research conducted on Hispaniola to date, but there is sufficient evidence to suggest the general patterns of archaeological remains.

While many prehistoric sites are known on Hispaniola, there have been few systematic settlement surveys on the island. Rainey and Rouse surveyed the area around Fort Liberté in Haiti in the 1930s; Bullen and Bullen (1979) made a partial reconnaissance of the lands held by Gulf and Western on the southeastern coast; Ortega (1978) surveyed a section of coastline at Macao, on the eastern tip of the island; and Veloz Maggiolo and Ortega (1980) conducted regional research in an area on the north coast of the island. At present, however, it is not possible to construct on Hispaniola as detailed a compilation of settlement types (or of numbers of settlements for each ceramic phase) as Rouse was able to do for Puerto Rico (Rouse 1948; Alegría 1965).

Nevertheless, some broad characteristics of Taíno sites can be suggested. Open-air villages of one to two hectares (2–5 acres) with ten or less large dwelling structures seem to be the most common (Veloz Maggiolo 1972). These structures are represented by separate or coalesced midden deposits. In many of these sites, the refuse mounds surround an open area or plaza like those mentioned in the historical accounts (chapters 2–4). Such sites are found both on the coast and inland, especially in areas with productive agricultural land. Similar kinds of sites have been found in eastern Cuba (Rouse 1942).

Taíno burials are found in three contexts (Morbán Laucer 1979; Veloz Maggiolo 1972; Rouse 1948). They occur in the village middens as primary or secondary inhumations, with the body in a variety of flexed, bundled, extended, or sitting positions. Infants are often interred in ceramic vessels within the middens. The second context, within which Taíno burials were first recognized, is in caves (Boyrie de Moya 1960). The burials in caves seem to have been accorded higher status than those in middens: the caves are often decorated with petroglyphs and often are partially blocked by stones at the entrance. Since most of the island is composed of metamorphic rocks in which caves do not occur, the tombs are sometimes dug into the sides of cliffs. Most cave burials contain more than one individual and fewer than twenty (p. 69). The third burial context is in "cemeteries," or areas near settlements apparently reserved for the burials, such as the site of La Union, near Puerto Plata on the north coast of Hispaniola (Veloz Maggiolo et al. 1972). The cemetery was located 225 m (740 ft) west of an apparently associated habitation site and contained twenty burials. They exhibited no regular orientation or body position. The ceramics found in the occupation middens near La Union were of both the Meillacoid and Chicoid series, but in the five burials that contained pottery, the vessels found were all of the Chicoid series. Veloz Maggiolo et al. (1972:143) note that in comparison with the Chicoid-period cemeteries in southeast Hispaniola, the burials at La Union have very few and very plain funerary goods.

An important class of Taíno construction for the present study is that of sites containing one or more specially constructed ceremonial plazas called "bateyes," "corrales," or "ball courts" (Alegría 1983; Veloz Maggiolo 1972). These constructions are related to similar structures throughout South America, Mesoamerica, and southwest North America. In the Caribbean, ball courts vary in size and construction but generally consist of a rectangle, oval, or circle of level ground surrounded by earth embankments usually about a meter in height. Typically, the structure might be 50 by 20 m (165 by 65 ft). The embankments are often (particularly in Puerto Rico [e.g. Ponce and Caguana]) faced with flat stone slabs, sometimes carved with petroglyphs. Other elaborations include stone pavings surrounding part of the court or, when there are several courts, leading between them (Alegría 1983).

The ceramics clearly associated with the ball courts are all of post-Saladoid ceramic types (Alegría 1979:5). On Puerto Rico they include the Ostiones, Santa Elena, Esperanza, and Capá styles (Rouse 1942), and on Hispaniola principally the Meillacoid and Chicoid ceramic styles (Veloz Maggiolo 1972). Accurate radiocarbon dates are almost nonexistent, but the ceramic chronologies would suggest that the ball courts were built and used from around A.D. 800 until the time of Spanish contact (Alvarado Zayas 1981). Where they are noted in the archaeological reports, the kinds of ceramics associated with specific ball courts on Hispaniola are shown in figure 3.

The ball courts were the sites of some of the *areyto*s and public rituals described in chapters 3 and 4. Probably all were also used for the ball game itself. In the game, two teams competed in trying to keep a ball from falling to the ground, using any part of their bodies except their hands. Las Casas (*Apologética* 1967:537) describes the game as follows:

> Twenty or thirty stood at either end of the long enclosure. Those at one end would toss the ball to those at the opposite extreme and it was then smitten by whoever was nearest: with the shoulder, if the ball flew high, which made the ball return like lightning; and if it flew close to the ground, quickly putting their right hand to the ground and leaning on it, they would smite the ball with the point of a buttock, which made the ball return more slowly. Those on the opposite side would likewise send it back with their buttock, until one or the other side committed a fault according to the rules of the game. It was a joyous sight to see when they played heated, especially when the women played with one another, they not hitting the ball with shoulder and buttock but with knees and I believe with their closed fists. (Alegría's translation, 1983:10)

Figure 3. Size and locations of ball courts on Hispaniola

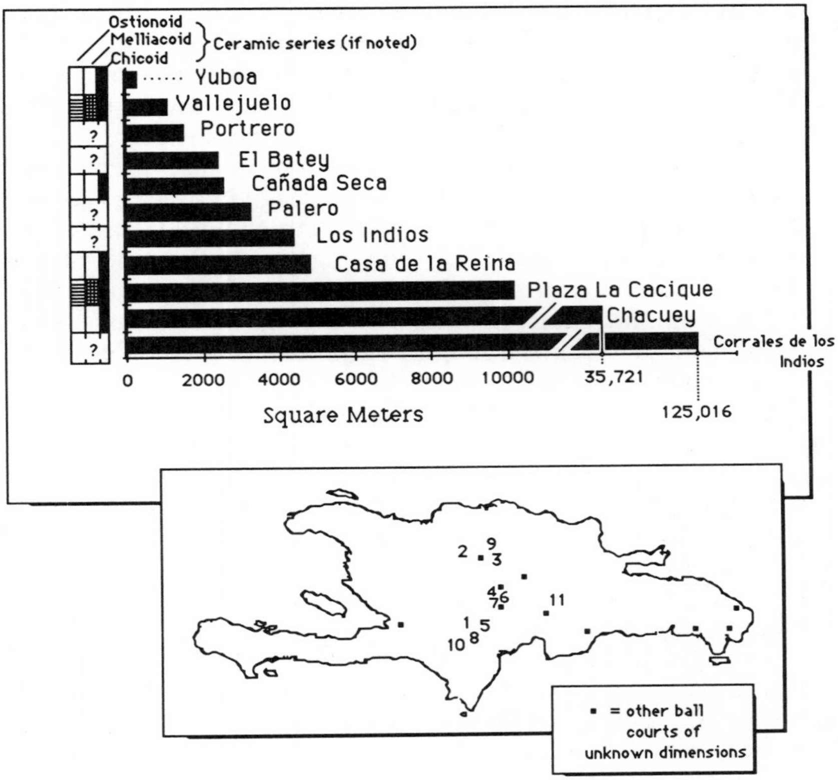

The ball game was a venue for interaction and competition between villages and larger polities and apparently had social and political ramifications that exceeded the Spanish observers' understanding. In one instance, for example, the game was played to decide the fate of a Spanish prisoner (Oviedo 1851, I:471). In this sense, the game seems to have provided a symbolic metaphor for or alternative to warfare and was a factor in the cohesion of federations of multivillage polities that are described in chapter 3 (Wilson 1985b).

Figure 3 shows the size and locations of twenty-one known ball courts from the island of Hispaniola. Figure 4 shows the locations of sixty-five ball courts from Puerto Rico and shows the contrast in size between those from Puerto Rico and from Hispaniola. The ball courts on Hispaniola are fewer than those on Puerto Rico—

only a third as many are known—and generally they are larger in size. Even if we disregard the immense circular construction at Corrales de los Indios on Hispaniola (probably the site of the cacique Caonabo; see chapters 3 and 4), the average size on Hispaniola is ten times that of Puerto Rico—6,605 vs. 642 m² (71,022 vs 6,903 ft²).

This observation may suggest that there are significant differences between the Taíno societies of Puerto Rico and Hispaniola. It is possible that the Taíno polities on Hispaniola were fewer and larger as well, a hypothesis that is supported by the documents dealing with the conquest of Puerto Rico (which started in 1509

Figure 4. Size comparison between ball courts on Hispaniola and Puerto Rico

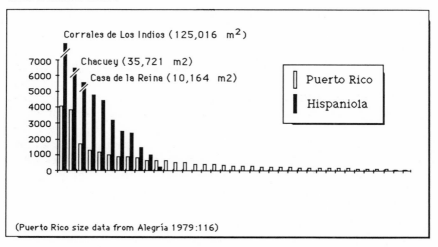

Corrales de Los Indios (125,016 m²)

Chacuey (35,721 m2)

Casa de la Reina (10,164 m2)

Puerto Rico

Hispaniola

(Puerto Rico size data from Alegría 1979:116)

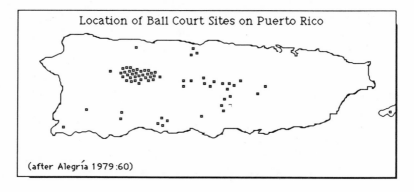

Location of Ball Court Sites on Puerto Rico

(after Alegría 1979:60)

[Brau 1966]). On the other hand, archaeological research on Puerto Rico has benefited from decades of financial support that Dominicano archaeology has lacked, and the disparity in number of sites may be partially due to accidents of discovery. Also potentially responsible for the disparity is the fact that many of the ball courts on Hispaniola are of earthen construction with minimal stone facings and thus are more easily destroyed by cultivation and erosion (Alegría 1983; Veloz Maggiolo 1972).

Another facet of Taíno material culture that is recoverable archaeologically includes items traded as prestige goods from polity to polity and island to island. Of the many trade goods that were reported to have been traded in the ethnohistorical accounts, only a few are preserved in archaeological contexts. Ethnohistorical accounts mention such items as parrots, feathers, raw and woven cotton, carved woods, gold, and *guanin* (a gold alloy) (Loven 1935). Esoteric knowledge, that which characterized a cacique in Helms's (1980, 1988) sense, is also mentioned, as in the gift of an *areyto*, or sacred song, in chapter 3.

The trade objects that are most evident archaeologically are the elaborate Chicoid ceramics, such as anthropomorphic and zoomorphic effigy bottles, and carved stone objects. Chicoid ceramics, probably from Hispaniola, appear as trade items in Cuba, Jamaica, Puerto Rico, and the Bahamas (Alegría 1976; Veloz Maggiolo 1972). They are often marked with repetitive and highly stylized artistic motifs suggesting that the goods possessed a greater and more specific symbolic content than that of goods that simply marked social status (García Arévalo 1983, for example, discusses the common appearance of bat motifs that occur on vessels used as grave offerings).

On Puerto Rico, carved stone objects were important trade items that have survived archaeologically. Especially valued were elaborately carved "trigonolito" *zemi*s—triangular stones carved with human or animal faces within which dwelled supernatural spirits (Arnáiz 1983; Arrom 1967, 1975; Chanlatte Baik 1985; Olsen 1974a, 1974b; Sued Badillo 1978). The *zemi* spirits allied themselves with specific caciques as long as they received the appropriate propitiation. Another class of stone items found principally on Puerto Rico are associated with the ball game. These are the spectacularly carved stone "belts" and "elbow stones"— partial belts which were used in conjunction with perishable materials (Alegría 1983; Ekholm 1946; Rouse 1964).

Because of the obvious correspondences the Taíno shared with mainland cultures (ball courts, stone belts, ceremonial axes, caciques carried on litters, the artistic representation of animals not found in the Caribbean, etc.), diffusion arguments have always been a part of Caribbean archaeology. It is impossible to argue the case that the Taíno emerged and lived in complete isolation. The Indians of the Lesser and Greater Antilles are historically related to South American groups, and as Rouse (1986) has argued, the sea was less a hindrance than an asset to long-distance travel. Similarities are therefore to be expected. Moreover, in the Lesser Antilles at least, interaction with mainland South America continued into the conquest period.

Of the three possible directions of interaction—South America, Mesoamerica, and southeast North America—it is clear that the most significant source for extra-Caribbean contact was South America (Allaire 1980; Boomert 1985; Sanoja Obediente 1983; Veloz Maggiolo 1972). The importance of possible contacts with the other two regions, however, continues to be a matter of debate.

Sturdevant (1960) provides an exhaustive review of potential contacts between Caribbean islands and the North American southeast. He concludes that "the supposed ethnological parallels between the Southeast and the Antilles are either nonexistent or can be explained on grounds other than diffusion across the Straits of Florida. The good parallels which exist are few enough so that they may be 'purely fortuitous'" (1960:43). Keegan (1987) has reviewed the arguments for contact between the Caribbean and southern Florida, especially those suggesting that the maize found in southern Florida was of South American origin, via a diffusion route through the Antilles (Sears 1977, 1982). Keegan and Diamond (1987:71) argue that while travel to the Florida peninsula would have been relatively easy for Caribbean islanders, competition with people living on the mainland prevented extensive interaction or colonization there.

The ethnohistorical evidence for contact with Mesoamerica is scant—the mention in a version of the Popul Vuh of a possible attack by Caribbean Indians, and the comment in Bernal Diez's history of the conquest of Mexico that there was a Jamaican woman on Cozumel. Rouse (1958, 1966) provides a comprehensive review of the ethnohistorical, linguistic, and archaeological evidence for interaction with Mesoamerica, concluding that the evidence for interaction between the two areas is "suggestive but not conclusive." Rouse (1966:236–37) catalogs several instances of Mesoamerican artifacts that were reported from the Caribbean, in each case with uncertain provenience. Since the publication of his article, to my knowledge, no more positive evidence has accrued to support the interpretation that there was extensive contact between the Caribbean and the Central American or Mesoamerican mainland (despite continual arguments, made on stylistic grounds, that such contact did exist and was significant in the development of Taíno society; e.g. García Goyco 1984).

The formal similarities between the societies of the Caribbean and those surrounding it remain a troubling problem. The maritime technology of the Taíno described by the Spaniards—canoes that could carry fifty to one hundred people (Rouse 1966:235–36) —indicates that there was no natural barrier to contact. The distances to mainland Florida or Yucatán are only slightly greater than those of voyages that would have been routine for Caribbean, Mesoamerican, or Southeastern mariners (Keegan and Diamond 1987). It must be concluded, however, that the technological or sociopolitical impact of whatever contact may have existed is not clearly manifest in Taíno culture.

Ethnohistorical Research on the Taíno

In the nearly five hundred years since the European conquest of the New World began, a great number of articles and books have appeared which deal in some fashion with the historical accounts of the Indians of the Greater Antilles. As could be anticipated, the body of writings that could be considered "ethnohistorical" are highly uneven in historiographical quality and insight.[2] Contrary to the logic that older accounts might be more accurate, since they are closer to the events in question, most of the well-researched historical studies have been made in the last century. Prior to the publication of transcriptions of the principal documents, it was impossible to conduct exhaustive historical research without extensive archival research in Spain and Italy. Las Casas's *Historia de las Indias* was not widely available until 1875, and his *Apologética historia sumaria* appeared only in 1909. Another indispensable resource is the forty-two-volume collection of docu-

---

[2]In Spores's definition (1980:575–76), "ethnohistory" constitutes an ethnological study based on historical documents.

ments combed from the Archivo General de las Indias in Sevilla. These were published between 1864 and 1884 as the *Colección de documentos inéditos relativos al descubrimiento, conquista, y organización de las antiguas posesiones españolas de América y Oceanía*.[3]

Most of the histories produced prior to the mid-nineteenth century, then, relied heavily on the journal and letters of Colón, on Oviedo's *Historia*, and on various versions of Martyr's *De Orbe Novo*. (Pierre François Xavier de Charlevoix's 1731–33 *Histoire de L'isle Espagnole ou de S. Domingue* is a well-researched exception.)

Another factor limiting ethnohistorical research on the Indians of the Greater Antilles involves the intellectual context in which the histories were written. The discipline of anthropology arose in the nineteenth century in part from the desire to understand non-Western cultures. The early historical studies which emphasized the Indians of the Antilles over the Spanish colonial experience emerged in the same social context and with the same broad motivations. The first works taking up the study of the Indians include Cornilliac (1875), Roth (1887), and Emile Nau's *Histoire des caciques du l'Haití* (1894).

The main body of historical sources pertinent to the conquest period became widely accessible in the early twentieth century, a period dominated by particularistic anthropological and historical methods. By midcentury a number of works had organized the principal historical documents into synopses of social and material cultural traits (Fewkes 1970 [1907]; Harrington 1921; Krieger 1930; Loven 1935; Herrera Fritot 1936; also Roth 1887 was organized in this way). Among the most thorough catalogs of both the historical documents and previous analyses of them, and a milestone in the study of the Caribbean Indians in this century, is Rouse's summary of existing knowledge about the Arawak and Caribs (1948).

Rouse's papers on the Arawak and Caribs have to some degree influenced nearly all of the subsequent studies, including the present one. Some of the best-known works containing ethnohistorical

---

[3]An additional twenty-five volumes (less important for this study) appeared between 1885 and 1932 as *Colección de documentos inéditos relativos al descubrimiento, conquista, y organización de las antiguas posesiones espanõlas de ultramar.*

information about the Taíno, such as Sauer's *The Early Spanish Main* and many others (Pichardo Moya 1956; Veloz Maggiolo 1972; Cassá 1974; Dreyfus 1981; Moya Pons 1983), rely to a great extent on Rouse's 1948 synthesis.

Subsequent ethnohistorical and archaeological research has pursued a variety of themes, many of which are raised elsewhere in this study. Helms (1980), Dreyfus-Gamelon (1976), Keegan and Maclachlan (1989), and Moscoso (1978) have discussed succession and inheritance among the Taíno. Arrom (1967, 1971), Alegría (1978), and Sanoja Obediente (1983) have tried, via comparison with mainland societies, to reconstruct aspects of Taíno mythology and cosmology, and Tavares (1978) has provided interpretations of other Taíno symbolic and cultural structures.

Three recent attempts to consider the Taíno within the conceptual context of evolutionary-stage schema are those of Dreyfus (1981), Alcina Franch (1983), and Cassá (1974). Their considerations of the place of the Taíno in worldwide comparative contexts is indicative of the present state of ethnohistorical thought on the Indians of the Caribbean. It represents, I think, an international group of scholars seeking to define a focus for research—to define the broad terms of a debate concerning the meaning of the Taíno in an intellectual atmosphere where very little consensus exists.

Dreyfus explores the comparison between the Caribbean and Polynesian chiefdoms, looking for similar historical motivations for cultural changes.

> One might draw a certain analogy in contrasting the social forms of the Greater and Lesser Antilles with those of the Polynesian islanders and the inhabitants of Melanesia. The ascension of the Carib war chief, the precariousness of his power, the constitution of his clientele through his network of kinship and intermarriage, are not unlike the "big men" institutions of Melanesia. In the Greater Antilles, by contrast, the hierarchical distribution [emboîtements hiérarchisés] of territory, the inheritance of statuses, the special etiquette with which Taíno chiefs are treated, and the importance attributed to their ancestral spirits and their genealogy all afford comparison with the Hawaiians. And it is not purely coincidence that "the impressive development of the taro culture on Hawaii," "the multiple ecological specializations in agricultural techniques, the different types of taro cultivation: mountain taro, wet taro, and, in the marécages, the *chinampa*-like taro plots" (Sahlins 1976:192–3), are developments that are equivalent to the intensification of manioc cultivation on Hispaniola. (1981:239)

Alcina Franch, in contrast to Dreyfus's representation of the Taíno as Hawaiian-like complex chiefdoms, takes the position that the Taíno were less than "chiefdoms" in a formal, definitional sense. His argument takes its definitions of "tribes" and "chiefdoms" from Service (1971), Fried (1967), Flannery (1975), and Sanders and Price (1968), while applying a materialistic theory of culture drawn from Harris (1982).

> The existence, in Taíno society, of a generalized concept of communal ownership of land; of a diffuse settlement pattern in which next to "urban" or "semi-urban" concentrations there is a dispersed population in very small settlements; of the absence of slavery, specialist artisans, full-time warriors, or priests; the absence, equally, of an agricultural system that permits the accumulation of surplus (except in the final epoch, immediately before the arrival of the Spanish) that came with more sophisticated techniques of cultivation—mounds and irrigation techniques—and the absence, finally, of a system of priestship [sistema sacerdotal] with temples and divinities, makes us think that it is necessary to define a type of society or level of sociocultural development of a transitional nature between tribes and chiefdoms in the proper sense, which in general terms corresponds to the proposed tropical or proto-theocratic mode of production, or to the "composite community" of the pre-Columbian mode of production. (1983:78–79)

Roberto Cassá also comments on the typological issue raised by the Taíno.

> Schematically, [the Taíno] can be located in the advanced Neolithic age; at a level which, in the classification of Morgan and Engles, can be seen as the last stages of barbarism, with the pattern of extended families; in the terms of Malinowski, in the class of allied village communities; following the modern sociological classification made by the Soviet historians, in the class of developed clan communities; and in agreement with the Mesoamerican classification of cultures, in the late archaic, with variations in the level of development. (1974:21–22)

Underlying these and a great many other differences in interpretation, however, a general consensus exists concerning the Taíno as described in the ethnohistorical material from the conquest period. Obvious points of similarity can be found in the various ethnohistorical descriptions of material traits (since ethnohistorians must draw their information from the same textual passages). Be-

cause the social and political organization of the Taíno is emphasized in the narrative chapters, this section examines these aspects
of Taíno society in particular.

While there is disagreement concerning the boundaries of political units (Vega 1980), it is agreed that the Taíno possessed a political organization uniting many villages under a central authority.
According to Rouse,

> Each province had its own chief, called a "cacique." In addition
> there are said to have been some 30 subchiefs in control of large dis-
> tricts within each province and 70 to 80 headmen in charge of the
> villages in the province.
>
>   Each chief, subchief, or village headman seems to have governed
> the village in which he resided. He organized the daily routine or
> work, arranging for hunting, fishing, and tilling the soil. He was also
> responsible for the storage of extra provisions and for their ultimate
> distribution among the villagers. His was the largest canoe in the vil-
> lage and he probably directed transportation. He acted as host to
> visitors and conducted relations with other villages, through their
> chiefs, subchiefs or headmen. (1948:528—29)

Both Cassá and Veloz Maggiolo modify this view slightly, arguing for a more informal hierarchy of subunits, with less definite
centralized authority (Cassá 1974:123), and for the absence of
a formal system of tribute, although the caciques' ability to demand labor is accepted (Veloz Maggiolo 1972:235).

The caciques were accorded special treatment (Dreyfus 1981;
Roth 1887:266); they lived in specially constructed houses, were
sometimes carried on litters, and in one historical instance addressed others only through two elderly men (the similarity to
Polynesian "speaking chiefs" has not been missed by those pursuing analogies with the Polynesian sociopolitical systems; see Dreyfus 1981; Helms 1980). The caciques and apparently other members of the elite practiced polygyny, having as many as thirty wives
(chapters 3 and 4). Also, the chief was given special burial considerations (chapter 4).

Within the body of ethnohistorical research on the Taíno, there
is agreement concerning the existence of four categories of social
status. Rouse's expression of this consensus is that

> beneath the set of chiefs was a hierarchy of other social classes
> which the Spaniards called nobles, commoners, and slaves. The no-
> bles (nitaynos) acted as the chief's assistants; for example, they su-

pervised communal labor. . . . They also had certain unspecified judicial functions. The commoners, for whom no native name is given, did the actual work of the village. In this they were assisted by the slaves (naborias), whose exact status is not known. (1948:530)

Cassá (1974), as noted above, disagrees with the characterization of *naborias* as slaves (see especially Moscoso 1983), and the significance of the *nitaínos* is not agreed upon, there being few historical references to this social category (Sauer 1966). The tiers of Taíno social status perceived by Spanish obeservers and the tiers of social status which existed in Spanish society are remarkably similar (Floyd 1973; Pike 1972), making it possible that the observers were projecting their own social organization on Taíno society.

The kinship system of the Taíno, either for elites or commoners, is unclear. Rouse (1948:531, following Roth 1887:266, who apparently takes the idea from Thurn 1887) states that inheritance was matrilineal but that residence patterns were patrilocal (Cassá 1974:141 and Veloz Maggiolo 1972:235 concur without discussion). Sued Badillo, arguing for the existence of female caciques, concludes:

The Taíno . . . were organized in matrilineal lineages which determined inheritance, residence, and succession. Each social unit traced itself to a common maternal ancestor. It was this maternal nexus (which cannot be confused with matriarchy) which established the group solidarity. Members of the same lineage very probably could not marry one another according to rules of exogamy. At the level of the political elite, the members took on public tasks hereditarily and without sexual discrimination.

Taíno society was a patriarchal society, but the succession to power was governed by one's maternal ancestry; the brothers and the sons of the sister of the cacique achieved power and not the paternal sons and nephews. When brothers or maternal nephews did not exist, the sisters and their daughters of the same lineage acceded. Thus succession was determined not on the basis of sex but on the basis of blood alone. (1985:19)

Sued Badillo's position seems to be based primarily on later conquest-period Puerto Rican material and contests other views of the position of women in Taíno sociopolitical structures (e.g. Alegría 1979).

Keegan and Maclachlan (1989) have argued that among the

Taíno elite, residence was viri-avunculocal—after marriage the couple would live in the village of the husband's mother's brother.

On present evidence, then, and in light of the interpretations just mentioned, it seems likely that the Taíno were a matrilineal society in which social status was transmitted through the matriline. The inheritance and succession of the title of cacique seems usually to have passed from a mother's brother to her son (the circumstances surrounding incidents of inheritance and succession are elaborated in chapters 3 and 4).

It seems possible, however, especially in light of the events discussed in chapters 3 and 4, that at least some qualities which were essential to accede to chiefship were transmitted through the patriline as well, i.e. from biological father to son.

In 1956 Goodenough commented on the difficulty in assessing a community's rules of residence in marriage, even when an ethnographer was there to conduct a house-to-house survey. Our task, in undertaking reconstructive ethnography from a biased and incomplete documentary record, is much more difficult and susceptible to error. The position taken here and expressed elsewhere (Wilson 1985a, 1985b, 1986) is that the patterns of kinship, residence, inheritance, and succession among the Taíno are more complex than we currently understand and involve conflicting and overlapping principles of marriage, inheritance, and succession. In particular, we must acknowledge that residence, succession, and broader aspects of Taíno social organization (e.g. the existence of clan or moiety structures not clearly understood at present) may have been quite different for the elite and nonelite segments of Taíno society. These problems, which are extremely important in understanding the structure and functioning of the Taíno chiefdoms, are taken up in the narrative chapters of the book and in the conclusions.

2

✳✳✳✳✳✳

The First Spanish Voyage to the New World

In the fifteenth century, Seville and Lisbon emerged as centers for merchants and traders trying to extend Europe's long-range trade routes in new and more profitable directions. The traditional eastern orientation of Mediterranean businessmen was threatened by increasing pressure on the spice roads by the Turks. At the same time, the exploration of the West African coast by the Portuguese offered a profitable alternative to the difficult Asian trade (Braudel 1972–74; Pike 1966, 1972; Sauer 1966).

The trading families of the city-state of Genoa were especially damaged by Turkish incursions on their eastern colonies and were faced with trade orientations shifting from east to west. Individually, the Genoese families employed a historically successful response to competing possibilities by diversifying; they sent representatives to live in many trading ports in the known world, including the trading centers of Andalusia. By the end of the fifteenth century, there were large and growing colonies of Genoese in Seville and Lisbon (Pike 1966:1–6). They were involved in a wide range of commercial activities, including moneylending and the short-distance trade of grain. They also continued to pursue long-distance trade to the east and north, taking advantage of the pivotal location of Seville and Lisbon between the Atlantic and Mediterranean markets. Their ships traveled from the tip of Africa to Iceland.[1]

---

[1] In 1477 Cristóbal Colón, who had been at sea for 16 years, sailed from Lisbon to Iceland and later to Africa's Gold Coast (Morison 1942:24–25).

Lisbon and Seville in the late fifteenth century were also markets for venture capital—money that could be invested in high-risk but potentially high-return enterprises (Floyd 1973; Pérez de Tudela 1983; Pike 1972). The Portuguese success in West Africa reinforced the belief that vast wealth accrued to those who opened up new markets and managed to retain some control over their exploitation. A good example was the fortified trading factory of São Jorge da Mina in Ghana, established by Don João II of Portugal in 1481 (Braudel 1972–74, 1982). Don Diogo d'Azambuja headed the expedition and directed the construction of a castle at the place now called Cape Coast. In 1481, São Jorge da Mina was near the forward edge of Portugal's exploratory thrust down the African coast, and it represented a considerable risk on the part of the Portuguese princes and the explorers themselves. Although the ships never left sight of land, the 5,500-km (3,400 mi) voyage to São Jorge da Mina was nearly as long as the 6,400-km (4,000 mi) trip to the New World.

An ambitious Genoese sailor named Cristóbal Colón may have participated in d'Azambuja's 1481 expedition (Morison 1942). In any case, Colón visited São Jorge da Mina shortly after its founding. On this and similar voyages for Portuguese entrepreneurs or for the Portuguese crown, Colón gained experience in sailing unknown coasts and in dealing with non-European people.

Colón and Toscanelli

Colón's personal ambition to sail west across the Atlantic dated to before the trip to the Gold Coast. His remarkable correspondence with the Florentine geographer and astronomer Paolo Toscanelli was going on in the 1470s and ended with Toscanelli's death in 1482. In the seafaring countries of the Mediterranean and Europe, Toscanelli was considered one of the foremost experts on geography and navigation in the period (Markham 1893; Morison 1942; Todorov 1984; Vignaud 1902). Toscanelli combined his calculations of the shape and size of the world with a careful reading of the accounts of the Far East that had been trickling westward with the spice caravans since the thirteenth century. Combining the classic geographic reconstructions of Ptolemy, and including the evidence of Marco Polo's accounts of his expedition to China of the 1270s (and Polo's uncles' trip of the 1260s), Toscanelli produced a map of the world and estimates of the distance between Portugal and the lands described by the Polos.

In reply to Colón's request for information Toscanelli's letter begins as follows:

> Paul, the Physician, to Cristobal Colombo greeting. I perceive your magnificent and great desire to find a way to where the spices grow, and in reply to your letter I send you the copy of another letter which I wrote, some days ago, to a friend and favourite [Hernán Martínez] of the most serene King of Portugal before the wars of Castille, in reply to another which, by direction of his highness, he wrote to me on the . . . subject [of sailing west from Portugal to reach the East Indies], and I send you another sea chart like the one I sent him, by which you will be satisfied respecting your enquiries. (Columbus 1893:4)

So the information which Colón received about the western route to China was by no means his alone. Toscanelli was well respected, and his reconstruction of the world was the one most commonly accepted by navigators and educated people (Ballesteros y Beretta 1945; Vignaud 1902). His letter to Hernán Martínez and, through him, to the nephew of Prince Henry the Navigator and king of Portugal (Alfonso V) contains rather explicit sailing instructions.

> I, therefore, send to his Majesty a chart made by my own hands, on which are delineated your coasts and islands, whence you must begin to make your journey always westward, and the places at which you should arrive, and how far from the pole or the equinoctial line you ought to keep, and through how much space or over how many miles you should arrive at those most fertile places full of all sorts of spices and jewels. . . .
>
> From the city of Lisbon due west there are 26 spaces marked on the map, each of which has 250 miles, as far as the most noble and very great city of Quinsay [modern Hangzhou]. . . . But from the island of Antilia, known to you, to the most noble island of cippangue [Cipangu, or Japan] there are ten spaces. For that island is most fertile in gold, pearls, and precious stones, and they cover the temples and palaces with solid gold. Thus the spaces of sea to be crossed in the unknown parts are not great. Many things might perhaps have been declared more exactly, but a diligent thinker will be able to clear up the rest for himself. (Columbus 1893:4, 8–9)

Toscanelli's estimate of a distance of 8,000 km (5,000 mi) between the Portuguese coast and Japan missed by about 16,000 km (10,000 miles), but it was close enough to the 6,400 km (4,000 mi) distance from Seville to the Caribbean islands that it compounded Colón's confusion when he arrived in the Bahamas. On October 21, 1492, only ten days after reaching land in the New World, Colón recorded in his journal,

> I shall then shape a course for another much larger island, which I believe to be Cipango, judging from the signs made by the Indians I bring with me. They call it *Cuba*, and they say that there are ships and many skilled sailors there. Beyond this island there is another called *Bosio*, which they also say is very large, and others we shall see as we pass, lying between. According as I obtain tidings of gold or spices I shall settle what should be done. I am still resolved to go to the mainland and the city of Guisay [Toscanelli's "Quinsay"] and to deliver the letters [of greeting] of your Highnesses to the Grand Can, requesting a reply and returning with it. (Columbus 1893:55)

Although Colón's perception of the geography of the New World was distorted for the next decade, Toscanelli's backing reinforced Colón's desire to focus his efforts on the western oceans. It also lent the legitimacy of Toscanelli's name to his search for venture capital. In calculating the distance between Lisbon and Cipangu, however, Colón's underestimates were even more egregious than Toscanelli's. Colón figured that there were about 3,700 km (2,300 mi) between the Canaries and Japan (Morison 1942:65–70). His questionable mathematics, together with a widespread distrust of Marco Polo's stories by some educated Europeans, probably destroyed his chances of having the Portuguese government fund his first voyage. His 1484–85 request—three caravels, supplies, a title that would remain in his family perpetually, and a share of the profits—was turned down by Don João II.

Colón Secures Spanish Support for a Westward Voyage

In 1486, Colón turned his attention to the court of the Catholic sovereigns Ferdinand of Aragon and Isabela of Castille. His arrival in Seville was promising; he met and persuaded the count of Medinaceli, Don Luis de la Cerda, of the practicality and potential profits of his expedition, and the count wanted to fund the enterprise immediately. The matter was referred to the court of Ferdinand and Isabela, who also took an interest in Colón but who were absorbed with the final battles of the *reconquista* of the Iberian peninsula from the Moors. The crown sent the business to committees for consideration, where Colón tried to meet the familiar criticisms concerning his calculations about the width of the western ocean. The decision was tabled for several years.

In 1488, Colón turned back to Don João II of Portugal, with whom he still had good relations. In the previous year, however, Don João's captain Bartolomé Días had rounded the tip of southern Africa, and Portugal had its own very profitable avenue of exploration to pursue.

While Colón was petitioning the courts of Andalusia, his brother and partner Bartolomé was doing the same in England and France. This is the first reference to Bartolomé we have from the chronicles and histories of the discovery. In many respects, Bartolomé was the more capable of the two. Las Casas describes Bartolomé as follows:

> Here was a man who was prudent and very brave, and more calculating and astute than he appeared, and without the simplicity of Cristóbal. He had a Latin bearing and was expert in all of the things of men, extraordinarily wise and experienced in the ways of the sea. I believe that he was no less learned in cosmography and related things and in making navigational charts and globes and other things of that art than his brother, and I presume that in some of these things Bartolomé exceeded him, although he learned these things from Cristóbal.[2] He was taller than average in body, had a commanding and honorable appearance, although not as much as the Admiral. (Historia, I:153)

It is uncertain how far Bartolomé's negotiations with Henry VII progressed. Bartolomé's credentials were not impressive when he arrived in London in 1489 or 1490. In his nephew Fernando's biography, it is claimed that Bartolomé was attacked by pirates on the trip and arrived in London broke (Columbus 1824:36). Bartolomé's proposition was not rejected out of hand, however,

---

[2]In other accounts Cristóbal learned chartmaking from Bartolomé in the early 1470s in Lisbon (see Morison 1942:35–36).

and for the next few years he lived in England and France, trying to push his scheme through committees and making maps in France as a retainer of Charles VIII's elder sister.

Finally the Castillian siege of Grenada succeeded, and the war with the Moors was ended. This, it seemed, was what had held up Castillian support for Colón's expedition for a decade. But when Colón was summoned to Grenada (and provided with a generous allowance for travel and suitable clothes), it was to be for his greatest disappointment. Fernando's account of his father's rejection shows the real reasons why the matter was held up by so many years' deliberation.

> Columbus was so high in his demands of honour and emolument,
> requiring that he should be appointed admiral and viceroy of all the
> countries he might discover, together with other important conces-
> sions. The Spanish councilors deemed his demands too high to be
> granted, as too considerable even in the event of success; and, in
> case of disappointment, they thought it would reflect ridicule and the
> imputation of folly upon the court to have conceded such high titles.
> Owing to these considerations the business again came to nothing.
> (Columbus 1824:40)

Much more than the money, which he probably could have had from many other investors, Colón wanted extraordinary privileges and a perpetual title, which only the sovereigns could give. Rank and privilege were supremely important in fifteenth-century Andalusia, and the arrogance of Colón—the son of a Genoese weaver, aspiring to the title "Almirante del Mar Océano" (Admiral of the Ocean Sea)—offended Ferdinand and Isabela's courtiers tremendously. Yet Colón's audacity was matched by his charisma and powers of persuasion. He had powerful friends and called in what favors he had at this critical juncture. This made the difference; the recommendations of the advisers who decided against Colón were overruled by the direct petition of Colón's friends to the king and queen, and a contract was made with Colón.

Colón was very lucky that his bid for a title did not cost him a chance to reach the New World first. It was widely believed that Cipangu lay beyond the Atlantic Ocean; the only question was how far away it was. Except for Díaz's discovery that Africa could in fact be circumnavigated, Portugal would undoubtedly have sent a party to the west.[3]

---

[3]In fact, Portugal already had attempted an expedition beyond the known

Once the decision was made, things moved quickly. Colón went to the port of Palos with a document from the king and queen demanding that the town supply two outfitted caravels. This was to be Palos's punishment for what the king and queen called "certain things done and committed by you to our disservice" (Morison 1942:110). The two caravels were the *Niña* and the *Pinta*. Colón chartered the *Santa María* with the funds he had borrowed to contribute to the voyage. He apparently did not have much latitude in selecting ships, for the *Santa María* was too large and unwieldy for its purpose and always had trouble keeping up with the caravels.

A Palos family called Pinzón was instrumental in making the voyage possible. Las Casas calls them a family of "rich mariners and important people" in Palos (*Historia*, I:177). Martín Alonso Pinzón was captain of the *Pinta*, and his brother Vicente Yáñez Pinzón commanded the *Niña*. Several other Pinzóns appear on the lists of crews. The cooperation of the Pinzóns undoubtedly made it easier for Colón to recruit acceptable sailors in Palos. With their backing there was a greater sense that the expedition had a reasonable chance of returning, and even of making a profit. As it turned out, two of the three ships and fifty-two of the ninety men did return.

From Palos to the Bahamas

The three ships left Palos on August 3, 1492, and made for the Canary Islands, a voyage of about 1,300 km (800 mi). From August 12 until September 6, they stayed in the Canaries making repairs on the *Pinta*, refitting the *Niña's* sails, and loading stores and water. On September 9 they lost sight of the Canary Islands and continued west.

The explorers spent thirty-three days out of sight of land, turning the hourglass every half-hour, estimating their progress, making rudimentary observations of latitude and even more crude

---

islands of the Atlantic. Fernão Dulmo and João Estreito were given a commission in 1487 to sail beyond the Azores and find the island of Antilia, long rumored to lie farther west in the ocean. By leaving from the Azores, however, they missed the benefits of both the northeast trade winds and the north equatorial current moving from the Canaries to the Caribbean. Their two caravels sailed around in the high Atlantic for a few weeks and returned empty-handed.

guesses at their longitude. Understandably, a great deal of time was spent looking for signs of land. On September 14 Colón records in his journal that birds which never fly more than twenty-five leagues from land were sighted. On the sixteenth he saw "tufts of grass which were very green, and appeared to have been quite recently torn from the land" (Columbus 1893:24–30). On the seventeenth they found a live crab, and "very fine grass and herbs from rocks." On the eighteenth they saw a large cloud, "which is a sign of the proximity of land." On September 20 they saw a booby bird, or gannet, which they said never got more than twenty leagues from land, and the next day they saw a few more. On the twenty-first they saw a whale, "which is a sign that they were near land, because they always keep near the shore." Sightings of birds, grass, and crabs continued until September 25, when Martín Alonso Pinzón spotted land. Colón recorded the following:

> At sunset Martín Alonso went up on the poop of his ship, and with much joy called to the Admiral, claiming the reward, as he had sighted land. When the Admiral heard this positively declared, he says that he gave thanks to the Lord on his knees, while Martín Alonso said the *Gloria in excelsis* with his people. The Admiral's crew did the same. Those of the *Niña* all went up on the mast and into the rigging, and declared that it was land. (Columbus 1893:30)

At the time, however, they were as far as one can get from land in the central Atlantic, the nearest being about 3,200 km (2,000 mi) in any direction. That they were this far out of the normal European sailing waters was remarkable, given that almost all of the sailing of the time was done within sight of land. Long open-water voyages were not unknown, however. The Norse had found Greenland from Iceland, a trip of 400 km (250 mi) and had coasted south to mainland North America, settling Newfoundland (McGovern 1980). In the late 1430s and early 1440s, in voyages that were prototypes for the Columbian expedition, the Portuguese had discovered the lonely Azores, 1,600 km (1,000 mi) off the mainland. Colón probably sailed twice as far out of the sight of land as the next longest European voyage up to that time. His voyage rivals the amazing voyages of discovery in Polynesia, for which legs of 1,000 km (620 mi) and more away from land were routine (Keegan and Diamond 1987).

The search for signs of land continued, and Colón recorded

each sighting of birds. By October 10, 1492, they had been out of sight of land for more than a month, and despite the cosmographical arguments he had given the queen's committees, the pervading feeling that land might never be found even creeps into Colón's journal. The night of the tenth Colón stood on the highest part of the deck and thought he saw a light in the west. The next morning, a sailor on the *Pinta* spotted the first island.

The debate over which island was Colón's first landfall has been extensive and heated. Parker (1985) reviews over 250 years of discussion and competing claims concerning the landfall and rehearses in detail the arguments of twelve scholars for their respective landfalls and routes of passage through the Bahamas (Navarrete 1825; Irving 1828; Montlezun 1828; Becher 1856; Varnhagen 1864; Fox 1880; Murdock 1884; Morison 1942; Verhoog 1947; Link and Link 1958; Didiez Burgos 1974; Molander 1981). These twelve researchers (who represent the tip of the iceberg in terms of the scholarship that has been applied to the problem [see De Vorsey and Parker 1985; Gerace 1987]) suggest a total of eight possible landfalls, ranging from the island of Eleuthera on the north (Molander 1981) to Turks Island on the south (Verhoog 1947, see also Verhoog 1985). These two islands are about 720 km (450 mi) apart, suggesting both the possible range of the landfall and the scope of the disagreement concerning its location. Since Parker's review article other scholars have discussed the question (e.g. Judge 1986; Perez 1987; Gerace 1987).

The Bahamas are a collection of around seven hundred islands, banks, and cays that rise only a few dozen meters above the surface (figure 5). The shallow waters of the Bahamas are tricky to navigate, but it was fortunate that the ships' westerly course brought them into this line of islands, for they could steer north or south from their landfall with the trade winds. Beating from west to east against the wind proved to be difficult, especially for the ungainly *Santa María* (Morison and Obregón 1964).

Of the eight islands mentioned in Parker's (1985) review as possible landfalls (San Salvador [Watlings], Turks, Cat Island, Mayaguana, Samana Cay, East Caicos, Plana Cays, and Eleuthera) that might have been the expedition's landfall, none is very large: Eleuthera, with 518 km² (200 mi²) is the largest. Cat Island is about 389 km² (150 mi²); San Salvador (Watling Island), about 163 km² (63 mi²) in area; and Samana Cay, under 50 km² (20 mi²; island areas are from Keegan 1985:78).

Figure 5. The Bahamas

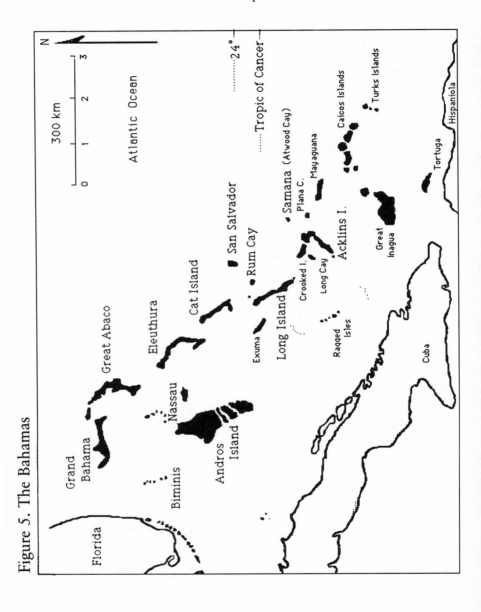

The question of which island Colón's group encountered first remains open, and its resolution will rely on interpretation of the somewhat cryptic observations in Colón's journal and on the reconstructions of modern navigators. I find it probable that the landfall was in the central Bahamas, between Cat Island and Mayaguana. Whatever island the ships landed upon, however, it was occupied by Indians who called it *Guanahaní*. They were similar in ancestry and culture to the people from the other islands.

The elaborate display the Spaniards put on when they landed was not proportional to the size of the island or the number of people there, but rather to the magnitude of the discoverers' dreams of glory. Colón's journal, as reproduced by Las Casas, describes the event.

> The Admiral . . . took weapons and went to shore in his armed boat, taking all the people it could hold. He also ordered Martín Alonso Pinzón and Vicente Yáñez. The Admiral took the royal banner, and the two captains carried banners with the green cross which they flew on their ships as their emblem—with an *F* which stood for the king Don Fernando, and an *I*, for the queen Doña Isabel, and above each letter a crown, one on one tip of the cross, one on the other.
>
> The Admiral and his party went on shore and fell to their knees, giving immense thanks to the all-powerful God, many shedding tears that they had been delivered safely, . . . especially Don Cristóbal Colon. . . . There the Admiral, in front of the two captains and Rodrigo de Escobedo, the secretary for the fleet, and Rodrigo Sánchez of Segovia, the royal *veedor* [witness, or inspector], and all of the men who had come to shore with him, . . . and before them all he took possession of the island and gave it the name San Salvador, for the king and for the queen, his lords, making the promises and statements that were required. (*Historia*, I:201)

The landing party planted their banners in the ground and took possession of the island in the name of Ferdinand and Isabela. It is not mentioned that the island and the people on it in no way matched Colón's expectations of what the Spice Islands of the Far East would be like. Marco Polo's tantalizing description of the island of Cipangu, or Japan, was quite different.

> Zipangu is an island in the eastern ocean, situated at the distance of about fifteen hundred miles from the main-land, or the coast of Manji. It is of considerable size; its inhabitants have fair complex-

ions, are well made, and are civilized in their manners. Their religion is the worship of idols. They are independent of every foreign power, and governed only by their own kings. They have gold in the greatest abundance, its sources being inexhaustible, but as the king does not allow of its being exported, few merchants visit the country, or is it frequented by much shipping from other parts. To this circumstance we are to attribute the extraordinary richness of the sovereign's palace. . . . The entire roof is covered with a plating of gold. . . . The ceilings of the halls are of the same precious metal; many of the apartments have small tables of pure gold, of considerable thickness; and the windows also have golden ornaments. (Marco Polo 1908:323–24)

Undoubtedly, Colón assumed that he was on some outlying islands from Cipangu or the mainland that the Polos had visited. Later he would try to sail west and find the realm of the Great Khan. In the meantime, he began to describe the people that were on this island. His descriptions (in Las Casas's *Historia*) of the people of *Guanahaní*, the indigenous name of the island, mirror his general assessment of all of the people he met on the first voyage.

The Indians, who were present there in great numbers, were astounded watching all of these actions by the Christians, and were taken aback by their beards, white skins, and clothes. . . . Along with those with him, the Admiral saw their simplicity, and with great pleasure and joy the Indians tolerated them; the Christians advanced to look at the Indians, no less amazed than the Indians were to look upon them; so great was their gentleness, simplicity, and confidence among people they had never known, despite their wild looks, and they could as easily have taken fright and fled from the Christians; it was marvelous how they walked among the Christians and were happy and were so natural and without fear or suspicion, as if they were fathers and sons; how they walked about as naked as when their mothers had bore them, with such nonchalance and simplicity. (*Historia*, I:202)

Colón describes the appearance of the inhabitants of *Guanahaní* as follows:

All that I saw were young men, none of them more than 30 years old, very well made, of very handsome bodies and very good faces; the hair coarse almost as the hair of a horse's tail and short; the hair they wear long and never cut. Some of them paint themselves black (and they are the color of the Canary Islanders, neither black nor white), and some paint themselves white, and others red, and others with what they have. Some paint their faces, others the whole body, others the eyes only, others only the nose. [from Morison's (1942:230) translation of Navarrete 1825]

Las Casas's transcription of Colón's journal continues,

They do not have weapons, or even know about them, because when shown a sword they grabbed it by the blade and cut themselves out of ignorance. They do not have any iron; their arrows are a kind without metal, and some of them have points made from the tooth of a fish, and others have other things. They are fairly tall and good looking, well made. They should be good and intelligent servants, and I believe that they could be converted into good Christians, for it does not appear that they have any other religion. (*Historia*, I:204)

The Indians of the Bahamas (or *Lucayos*, as the islands were known by their inhabitants) represented the northern limits of the expansion of Arawakan speakers into the Caribbean. From the archaeological evidence, it appears that people using Meillacan Ostionoid ceramics came north from the northern coast of Hispaniola around A.D. 800 (Keegan 1984, 1985; Keegan and Diamond 1987; Sullivan 1981). All the larger islands and cays in the Bahamas archipelago were colonized between A.D. 800 and the time of Spanish contact (Keegan and Maclachlan 1989).

The limestone plateau islands of the Bahamas are low and relatively dry. Most average 1,000–1,200 mm (40–47 in) of rain a year (Keegan 1985:90; Sears and Sullivan 1978:7), versus 1,700–2,300 mm (67–90 in) on the northeast coast of Hispaniola (Fuente Garcia 1976:165). The early inhabitants relied more on seafoods and less on the intensive cultivation of manioc than did the people of the Greater Antilles (Keegan 1986, 1988; Keegan and DeNiro 1988). Their villages were smaller and fewer than on the big islands, reflecting environmental constraints on production, scarcity of fresh water, and the strategy of colonization that the settlers employed (Keegan 1985).

Keegan's (1985) extensive settlement surveys of the Bahamas (and compilation of previous surveys) indicate that settlements— villages and smaller sites—are fairly densely distributed on the Bahamian islands. The larger sites, or "primate villages," tend to be located on the Leeward (western or northwestern) coasts, although exceptions exist (Keegan 1985, figs. 13–23; Sears and Sullivan 1978).

From the Bahamas to Cuba

Colón sailed around the southern end of the island and up the western coast, using the armed boat of the *Santa María* and the two ships' boats from the caravels. According to the account of Las Casas,

> There he began to see two or three villages and a large number of people, both men and women, who came down to the beach calling to the Christians and giving thanks to God. Some of them brought fresh water; others, things to eat; others, seeing that the boats were not going to land, dived into the water and came swimming out to the boats, and the sailors understood that the swimmers were asking for signs that they had come from the sky. (*Historia*, I:208)

Still coasting along the leeward side of the island, Colón observed six houses on a small peninsula, and above it "such beautiful green groves, that he took to be gardens, with much water, more gracious and beautiful than Castille in the month of May"(p. 208). Strangely, apart from the initial landing to take possession of the island for the crown, the boats did not land again on the island that was the first landfall. Colón claimed that he did not trust the reefs, but it appeared that he was hesitant to go among the people yelling from shore. The next morning, October 15, he set sail for one of the nearby islands and never saw San Salvador again.

Colón was determined to find the island of Cipangu and needed guides. On the day they took possession of San Salvador, Colón noted in his journal that "I, our Lord being pleased, will take hence, at the time of my departure, six natives for your Highnesses, that they may learn to speak" (Columbus 1893:38). The next day, he was getting some vague directions from the Indians about the location of the mainland, where the Spaniards were given to understand that there was gold in abundance. He understood them to say that "there was land to the S., to the S.W., and N.W., and that the natives from the N.W. often came to attack them, and went on to the S.W. in search of gold and precious stones"

(p. 40). Colón decided to steer to the southwest, where the gold seemd to be. "I tried to get [some of the Lucayan Indians] to go there," Colón notes, "but afterward I saw that they had no inclination" (p. 39). On the fourteenth he tells the king and queen in his narrative that

> these people are very simple as regards the use of arms, as your Highnesses will see from the seven that I caused to be taken, to bring home and learn our language and return; unless your Highnesses should order them all to be brought to Castille, or to be kept as captives[4] on the same island; for with fifty men they can all be subjugated and made to do what is required of them. (p. 41)

Of these seven captive guides, several escaped immediately, jumping overboard when the ships were near other islands. Through the voyage to Cuba and Hispaniola, some of these guides escaped and were replaced by people from where the Spaniards happened to be. One Indian, possibly from among the first group of seven taken from San Salvador, went back to Spain with the expedition (along with five others) and was baptized with the name Diego Colón. He accompanied the Admiral on the second voyage and figured prominently as an interpreter and liaison between the Spanish and the Taíno Indians.

In the early contact period, trade was the most important vehicle for interaction between the Spaniards and Indians. Trading began on the day the expedition arrived at San Salvador and Colón had taken possession of the island for the king and queen (October 11, 1492). After the landing party returned to the boat, many Indians came swimming out to the ships, "bringing us parrots, spun cotton in balls and spears and many other things; and we bartered with them for other things that we gave them, such as little beads of glass and cascabeles" (Las Casas, *Historia*, I:204). This exchange of small goods—symbols and proof of the other group's alien nature—dominated the trade in the Bahamas.

Similar events occurred at the island Colón called Santa María

---

[4]Colón uses the word "captivos" for captives rather than "esclavos" (slaves), but the idea that the islands could be a source of slaves, as the Portuguese had viewed their lands in West Africa, was present from the beginning. Within ten years Alonso de Hojeda led slaving raids in these islands, transporting the captives to Hispaniola.

de la Concepción (Rum Cay in Morison's reconstruction), but on the larger Long Island, which they reached on October 16, the Indians seemed to carry out these negotiations with more sophistication than they had on the smaller islands to the northeast. Colón observed that the people there were very similar to those on the other islands in language and customs but noted that "they appeared more domestic, with more business sense and more subtle, because they were more inclined to bargain about the prices and payment for the little things that they brought than the others we had seen until this time" (Las Casas, *Historia*, I:212).[5] This may have been because news of the Spaniards preceded them (as it certainly did) and the Indians were becoming accustomed to dealing with the foreigners. It may also be that the Spaniards, in trending to the south, were getting into areas of the Bahamas where more trade with the Indians of the Greater Antilles took place. From historic accounts from the island of Hispaniola and archaeological evidence in the islands the expedition first reached, we know that there was an active trade between the Greater Antilles and the Bahamas (Hoffman 1987; Keegan 1985; Sullivan 1981).

The Indians that they met first were accustomed to interisland trade. The trade items mentioned most are the skeins of spun cotton, which in the islands of the south were woven into capes and breechcloths. On San Salvador and Rum Cay, where cotton was offered in trade, the people did not wear such clothing.

On October 15, an event occurred which offers some idea of the interisland communication among the islands of the central Bahamas. The following is from Las Casas's transcription of the Admiral's journal:

> In the channel between the island of Santa María and the next, which was given the name Fernandina [Rum Cay and Long Island], they come upon an Indian alone in a little canoe. He carried some of the bread of those lands, called *cazabí* [cassava] . . . and a calabash of water and in a small basket some green leaves [contezuelas verdes] and two *blancas* [the smallest denomination of coins], the currency of Castille, from which it was known that he came from

---

[5]Las Casas's text: "Le parecía más doméstica y de más trato y más sotiles, porque los vía meor regatear sobre los precios y paga de las cosillas que traían que los que hasta entonces había visto."

San Salvador; having passed Santa María, he was heading for Fernandina to give them news of the Christians; having gone so far, and being alone in his little canoe, he was tired, so the Admiral brought both him and his boat on board. They gave him bread and honey and wine to drink, and when they were near to land, they gave him presents and sent him on his way with all of his possessions. (*Historia*, I:211)

The Spaniards' interpretation that this man was a messenger rather than a trader was probably accurate. Other accounts of trading missions represent much larger-scale projects, with canoes that carried more than forty people. The man in the canoe seemed to be carrying only two things beyond the basic necessities: the dried leaves were probably either tobacco or *cohoba* (a narcotic snuff), items used in rituals in which Taíno caciques and shamen communicated with spirits while in drug-induced trances; the coins were the man's proof that the strangers for whom he was the forerunner were truly unique in Caribbean experience. Coins are not mentioned as trade items on San Salvador but must have been one of the items the Spaniards left on the island.[6] The coins were also well suited to act as evidence of the Spaniards' extraordinary nature because Taíno metallurgy could not reproduce them and because they contained writing, other European symbols, and a style of representational art unknown in the Antilles (Tavares 1978).

With news of their coming preceding them, Colón took his ships southwestward through the Bahamas. On October 19 he sailed from Long Island to Crooked Island, which his guides called *Saomete* and Colón called Isabela. Along the way they saw a few small coastal villages, with hammocks hanging in the Lucayan houses, and encountered a species of dog that was indigenous to the New World (the mute or barkless New World dog). Coming around Crooked Island they spent the night of the nineteenth off of Fortune Island, which Colón called Cabo Hermoso. From his guides, Colón understood that there was a king on Fortune Island who had a great deal of gold. Even the Admiral was skeptical this time.

---

[6]Hoffman (1987) found a coin along with other European artifacts at the Long Bay site on San Salvador, a site which may have been the original landfall.

Tomorrow I intend to go so far inland as to find the village, and see and have some speech with this king, who, according to the signs they make, rules over all the neighbouring islands, goes about clothed, and wears much gold on his person. I do not give much faith to what they say, as well because I do not understand them as because they are so poor in gold that even a little that this king may have would appear much to them. (Columbus 1893:52–53).

The company stayed around Fortune and Crooked islands for a few more days, but the stories of the guides and the people who came to see the Europeans shifted to an island that they said was a day and a half's sail to the west-southwest from Crooked Island. From the reports he gathered, Colón was more sure than ever that this island the Indians called Cuba was in fact Cipangu. "I intended to go to the island of Cuba," Colón records on October 24, "where I heard of the people who were very great, and had gold, spices, merchandise, and large ships. . . . I cannot understand their language, but I believe that it is of the island of Cipango that they recount these wonders. On the spheres I saw, and on the delineations of the map of the world [which Paolo Toscanelli may have sent him], Cipango is in this region" (Columbus 1893:57). On October 25–26 the ships passed the Ragged Islands, a group of low islands that Colón called Las Islas de Arena. The islands must have been particularly unimpressive from the perspective of the ships, since these were the first islands not named for saints or royalty. They did not stop to take possession of the islands. On October 28, in heavy rain, they reached the north coast of the island the Indians called Cuba.

Like the Bahamas, eastern Cuba was one of the last areas colonized by the Arawakan speakers before European contact ended their migration through the Caribbean. Cuba had been occupied as early as 5000 B.C. by people who had a hunting and gathering economy, rather than the agricultural economy of the Arawakan speakers, and who did not make pottery (Veloz Maggiolo and Vega 1982; Koslowski 1978).

The Arawakan-speaking inhabitants of Cuba who met the discoverers apparently mentioned some non-Arawakan people called the *Guanahatabeys* and the *Guanahacabibes*. Formerly, the same peoples were called the *Ciboney* (Keegan and Maclachlan in press; Rouse 1986; Sauer 1966). It has been assumed that these people had been pushed westward or absorbed by the encroaching Taíno and that they still lived on the southwestern Guacayarima peninsula of Hispaniola and the western end of Cuba when the Europeans arrived (Rouse 1948; Sauer 1966). The identification of the ethnohistoric groups called *Guanahatabeys*, *Guanahacabibes*, and *Ciboney* with pre-Arawakan populations, and the assumption that they survived on Cuba and southwestern Hispaniola, has been challenged by Keegan and Maclachlan (in press) and Rouse and Moore (1983).

The archaeological sites of the aceramic, nonhorticultural Cubans are almost uniformly small coastal sites with a scatter of debris from their tools and food—fish, shellfish, iguanas, land and sea crabs, larger sea animals like the manatee and turtle, and land animals like the hutia (Rouse 1948:503–5).

The migration of people using Ostionan subseries ceramics reached eastern Cuba around A.D. 700 (Rouse 1986). Their archaeological remains and settlement preferences are very similar to those of the people who colonized Hispaniola, Jamaica, and the Bahamas. They grew manioc as a staple starch and complemented it with the kinds of terrestrial and marine foods that their nonhorticultural predecessors had collected. They located their settlements in places which would combine these components of their economy. The bays and rivers of northeast Cuba were ideal places for settlement, and as the three European ships sailed along the coast, they saw many of these villages.

The Taíno settlement in Cuba was strongly oriented to the east. They had strong ties of trade and social interaction with western Hispaniola, 83 km (52 mi) away across the Windward Passage. Nine of the ten ceremonial plazas or ball courts reported in the archaeological literature (Alegría 1983:16–27) are located near the eastern tip of Cuba, and the density of settlements was greatest in this part of the island.

Interaction with the Taíno on Cuba

Colón's ships reached Cuba on Sunday, October 28, and sailed into a bay which Colón named San Salvador. Following Morison's reconstruction of the first voyage (1942:254–55), their landfall was probably at Bahía Bariay. This bay is about 260 km (160 mi) northwest of the eastern tip of Cuba and was not densely populated in 1492. Colón made a reconnaissance of the bay in the *Santa María*'s armed boat and found only two houses. The occupants of the houses had fled, but among the things they left were nets, bone fishhooks, and fishing spears. The party concluded that this was merely a fishing camp for a larger inland settlement. Having fishing camps to catch and dry fish for shipment to inland settlements was practiced in the Greater Antilles, especially on Hispaniola, but in this bay the houses might just have been an isolated settlement.

On the twenty-ninth they sailed west about 13 km (8 mi) and found two more bays, the Río de la Luna and the Río de Mares. On the latter inlet, now called Puerto Gibara, they found a sizable village. Colón was anxious to find the more civilized parts of the Far East and the next day continued westward along the coast. His guides from the Bahamas continued to indicate that the cities the Admiral was searching for lay to the west, but the weather was not favorable, and the coast did not look any more promising as they headed west. On October 31 the wind shifted to the north and threatened a storm, so the company turned back for the shelter of Río de Mares.

Colón was more anxious than ever to find the Gran Khan and hoped for great things from Cuba. Instead, the Indians of Cuba were frustratingly similar to those of the other islands. The guides' assertions that Cipango was always just around the corner (although it was what Colón and the other captains also believed) had lost all credibility. On November 1 Colón wrote, "It is certain that this is the mainland, and that I am in front of *Zayto* and *Guinsay*" (Columbus 1893:65).

Zayto was the city Paolo Toscanelli had called Zaitun after Marco Polo's Zai-tun. The discrepancy between the account of Zai-tun given by Marco Polo and the reality of Cuba compounded the Admiral's frustration. Marco Polo describes the lands around Zai-tun (a port on the Chinese mainland across from the island of Taiwan) as follows:

> Upon leaving the city of Kan-Giu and crossing the river to proceed in a south-easterly direction, you travel during five days through a well-inhabited country, passing towns, castles, and substantial dwellings, plentifully supplied with all kinds of provisions. The road lies over hills, across plains, and through woods, in which are found many of those shrubs from whence the camphor is procured. The country abounds also with game. The inhabitants are idolaters. They are subjects of the grand khan, and within the jurisdiction of Kan-giu. At the end of five days' journey, you arrive at the noble and handsome city of Zai-tun, which has a port on the sea-coast cele-

brated for the resort of shipping, loaded with merchandise, that is afterwards distributed through every part of the province of Manji. . .

The country is delightful. The people are idolaters, and have all the necessaries of life in plenty: their disposition is peaceable, and they are fond of ease and indulgence. Many persons arrive in this city from the interior parts of India for the purpose of having their persons ornamented by puncturing with needles (in the manner before described), as it is celebrated for the number of artists skilled in that practice. (Marco Polo 1908:317).

Colón had to view this account critically. The veracity of Marco Polo's stories was not unequivocally assumed by educated Europeans, and Colón would have had to allow for some exaggeration.

In contrast to other travelers to the East, Marco Polo's was in fact a highly accurate portrait. The master of hearsay evidence, Sir John Mandeville, traveled to the Far East from 1322 to 1356 and described the islands of the East Indies in his *Travels*.

There are many different kinds of people in these isles. In one, there is a race of great stature, like giants, foul and horrible to look at; they have one eye only, in the middle of their foreheads. They eat raw flesh and raw fish. In another part, there are ugly folk without heads, who have eyes in each shoulder; their mouths are round, like a horseshoe, in the middle of their chest. In yet another part there are headless men whose eyes and mouths are on their backs. And there are in another place folk with flat faces, without noses or eyes; but they have two small holes instead of eyes, and a flat lipless mouth. In another isle there are ugly fellows whose upper lip is so big that when they sleep in the sun they cover all their faces with it. (Mandeville 1983:137)

Colón had apparently read Mandeville and referred to myths like those concerning the islands of the Amazon women. Stories of the isle of the Amazons had been repeated since before Herodotus, and in the journal from the first voyage, Colón reported that this island was in the Caribbean. Along with Toscanelli's interpretations, Polo was a more useful eyewitness in Colón's exploration of the Caribbean. Colón continued to believe that Cuba was part of the mainland for a decade after 1492 and that he could have found the Gran Khan if he had continued westward. But adverse winds and the pressures from his colleagues dictated that he proceed eastward.

The expedition's eleven-day stay in Río de Mares was an interesting one, from what can be told from Colón's journal. They needed the time to recover from their long voyage and their experiences in the Bahamas. The ships needed to be beached (one at a time, the Admiral insisted), scraped, and recaulked with mastic to seal their leaks. They needed to restock the supply of fuel for the cooking fires and try to collect some additional food. One of their passengers from San Salvador went ashore and described the things that these strangers gave away, and a brisk trade soon developed.

Colón still wanted to find the "towns, castles, and substantial dwellings" that Marco Polo described and determined to send two men inland for six days. He selected the two men on the basis of their diplomatic qualifications and language skills. Rodrigo de Xeréz had traveled to Africa on a Portuguese expedition and had been part of a mission inland to visit an African king. The other man was Luis de Torres, "who had lived with the Adelantado of Murcia and had been a Jew[7] and knew Hebrew and Chaldean and even spoke a little Arabic" (Las Casas, *Historia*, I:227). Las Casas continues:

> With these two he sent two Indians, one of the ones they had brought from Guanahaní [San Salvador] and the other from the settlements along the Río de Mares. He sent with them some strings of beads and other things to trade for food if they ran short, and gave them six days in which to return. He gave them samples of spices so that they would know them if they saw them. He gave them instructions to ask for the king of that land, and to speak on behalf of the king and queen of Castille, who had sent the Admiral to present them with their letters and a royal present. (Pp. 227–28)

The four men headed up the river valley carrying royal presents and letters of greeting from the king and queen of Castille to the Gran Khan. On the night of November 5, three days later, they returned with a story of what was very much a state visit from the Indians' perspective. They said that they had marched twelve leagues (about 64 km, or 40 miles) inland and had visited a large village. The two ambassadors' description of their encounter with

---

[7]He was probably a convert who had avoided the expulsion of the Jews from Spain in 1492.

the Taíno Indians matches those of later interactions so exactly that there is no doubt of the accuracy of their account.

> They came to a village of 50 houses, where there were a thousand inhabitants, for many live in one house. These houses are like very large booths. They said that they were received with great solemnity, according to custom, and all, both men and women, came out to see them. They were lodged in the best houses, and the people touched them, kissing their hands and feet, marvelling and believing that they came from heaven, and so they gave them to understand. . . . When they arrived, the chief people conducted them by the arms to the principal house, gave them two chairs on which to sit, and all the natives sat round them on the ground. The Indians who came with them described the manner of living of the Christians, and said that they were good people. Presently the men went out, and the women came sitting round them in the same way, kissing their hands and feet, and looking to see if they were of flesh and bones like themselves. . . . Finding that they had no information respecting cities, the Spaniards returned; and if they had desired to take those who wished to accompany them, more than 500 men and women would have come, because they thought the Spaniards were returning to heaven. (Columbus 1893:69–70)

They were met by the cacique of the village and taken to the *bohio*, the rectangular house of the chief, that was distinct from the rounded *caneys* of the commoners. They were seated on carved *lignum vitae*, or "ironwood" *dujos*, the ceremonial seats that were the most valued possession of the Taíno elite.[8] In the traditional Taíno formula of greeting for high-ranking visitors, they were given food as soon as they arrived (Las Casas, *Historia*, I:230). Las Casas is perhaps intentionally vague in describing the women's part in this ritual. He says:

> After a while all of the men left, and all of the women entered, and they seated themselves among the visitors, exactly as the men had

---

[8]Fernando Colón (1824) describes these seats in more detail: "They were seated upon wooden stools made of one piece, in very strange shapes, almost resembling some living creature with four very short legs. The tail was lifted up, and as broad as the seat, to serve for the convenience of leaning against; and the front was carved into the resemblance of a head, having golden eyes and ears" (Columbus 1824:120).

done, and all of them touched them and felt them to see if they were
of meat and bone like them, and they kissed their hands and their
feet, and they left nothing out in adoring them; they asked them insistently and with great urgency that they stay there and live with
them. (P. 230)[9]

Fernando Colón's biography of his father adds a detail to the
other's descriptions of the women's role in this episode. He says
that the women "offered them presents of various articles" (Kerr
1824:63). What presents the women gave Colón's two emissaries
is unknown, but the general pattern repeats itself in subsequent
interactions with elite Taíno women: the men would greet the visitors first and give them food; afterward the women and sometimes the men would give them presents of high-status goods with
symbolic value. This pattern will be seen again in the accounts
of the Adelantado Bartolomé Colón's trip to the province of Xaraguá on Hispaniola (chapter 4).

The two Spaniards brought out the dried specimens of Southeast
Asian spice plants (pepper and cinnamon) and asked their hosts
where they could find such plants. The answer was very much
like what they were told when they asked where the gold was:
"No, there is none around here, but they have a lot of it to the
southeast" (Las Casas *Historia*, I:230). They may have been refer-
ring to the southeastern tip of Cuba, or perhaps to the island
of Hispaniola. The two men also questioned the villagers as well
as they could about large inland cities, but it was obvious to them
that they were in the largest village around. The next-largest village they had passed on their hike inland had had only five houses.
So the explorers returned to the ships. The cacique of the village
walked back with them to the Río de Mares, together with his
son and another person.

By acting on the information and directions given him by all
the Indians he had met, Colón was closing in on what was, in
the Taíno frame of reference, the source of all good things—

---

[9]Las Casas's text: "Desde a un rato, saliéronse todos los hombres, y entraron
todas las mujeres, las cuales se asentaron alrededor dellos, como habían hecho
los hombres, y todas las que podían los tentaban y palpaban si eran de carne
y de hueso como ellos, y besábanles las manos y los pies, y no les faltaba sino
adorarlos; rogábanles con gran instancia e importunaciones que se quedasen
allí a vivir con ellos."

Hispaniola. "Today I got the ship afloat, and prepared to depart on Thursday, in the name of God, and to steer S.E. in search of gold and spices, and to discover land" (Columbus 1893:72).

He had news of another island that was due east of where they were on Cuba, one the Indians from the Bahamas called *Babeque*. This was Great Inagua Island, a stepping-stone between the Bahamas and Cuba that Colón had missed. Given the same reports of plentiful gold and spices by his guides, there was little reason to steer for Babeque instead of *Bohío* (the local name for Hispaniola). The difficulties of sailing directly into the easterly trade winds made it hard enough to get away from the northeast coast of Cuba. The course that Colón steered between November 12 and December 12 reveals both his indecision about which way they should head and his difficulties in pushing eastward. Martín Alonso Pinzón had neither problem: the agile *Pinta* could sail more easily into the wind, and Pinzón's guides argued persuasively that Babeque was where the gold was. On November 22 the *Pinta* took advantage of a southern breeze and headed for Grand Inagua, leaving the *Santa María* and the *Niña* behind.

Colón continued to sail in a southeasterly direction along the coast of Cuba for the next two weeks. They were held up by the weather for a few days in the large bay at Baracoa. On the eastern end of Cuba Colón comments several times on the number and size of the native canoes. On November 30 he records, "Near one river they saw a canoe dug out of a single tree, 95 *palmos* long, and capable of carrying 150 people" (Columbus 1893:93). A few days later,

> they came to a cove in which were five very large canoes, so well constructed that it was a pleasure to look at them. They were under spreading trees, and a path led from them to a very well-built boathouse, so thatched that neither sun nor rain could do any harm. Within it there was another canoe made out of a single tree like the others, like a galley with 17 benches. It was a pleasant sight to look upon such goodly work. (P. 94).

These large seagoing canoes were the vessels used for interisland visits and trade throughout the Caribbean. The largest and most ornate were as much statements of a cacique's power and prestige as they were a form of transportation. Smaller canoes carried out trade between the islands equally well and with fewer people (Nicholson 1976).

The Discovery of Hispaniola

Finally, on December 5, Colón caught a favorable wind and left Punta Maisí on the eastern tip of Cuba and sailed out into the Windward Passage. After sailing some distance from the shores of Cuba, the mountains of Haiti came into view in the southeast, and Colón decided to head for them. This was a most disturbing turn of events for the islanders from the Bahamas. They appeared to be terrified of the people of Hispaniola and told the familiar Caribbean stories about the cannibalistic nature of those people. It is not clear just what this means; they had had a similar reaction to landing on the northeast coast of Cuba and insistently promoted Babeque as the next port of call. They may have been looking for a way to get closer to their own islands before trying to escape from the foreigners. It is possible, however, despite the trade that apparently went on between the two areas (Keegan 1985; Sullivan 1981), that the coast of Hispaniola was a dangerous place for people coming down from the frontier of the Arawakan expansion.

The people on Hispaniola's coasts greeted the Spaniards with a great deal more reticence and suspicion than any of the other islanders had. When they landed at Puerto St. Nicolas, they saw signs of a large population, but nobody came down to greet them. Colón noted that "there must be many inhabitants, judging from the number of large canoes, like galleys, with 15 benches" (Columbus 1893:101). For several days they saw signal fires burning day and night. The guides from the Bahamas did not even want to come on deck, much less go walking off into the forest to explain themselves to these dangerous cannibals. Colón decided that waiting around to make contact with the people of Puerto St. Nicolas would take too long, so he headed eastward along Hispaniola's north coast.

After being on the coasts of Hispaniola for five days, they still had not had any contact with the islanders. Colón had decided that his guides' words for cannibals, *canibas* and *caribas*, meant *Khan*-ibas—soldiers of the Gran Khan. On December 10 he sent some of his men inland to make contact, but they returned empty-handed. On the twelfth some of the crew caught a woman who was in the forest near the shore with a group of people and brought her to the ship. Colón employed the method he had used with success before, giving her cascabeles and glass beads, then freeing her to spread the news of the foreigners' generosity. When no one arrived the next day, Colón sent an armed party inland to find the village. They walked up the valley of Les Trois Rivièrs and found a village "of a thousand houses, with over three thousand inhabitants" (Columbus 1893:108).[10]

The villagers fled when the party approached, but the guides chased them and explained that "the Christians were not from Caniba, but were from the sky, and they give lots of beautiful things to anyone they meet" (Las Casas, *Historia*, I:259). Two thousand villagers gathered around them and "put their hands on the Christians' heads, which was a sign of friendship and great reverence, and when they had done this they were all trembling until the Christians assured them" (p. 259). Some of the people went into the houses and brought out cassava bread and fish and many other things to eat. After the party had eaten, gifts were exchanged. The Indians had heard from the guides that Colón wanted parrots. Within the context of Taíno culture, this confirmed Colón's high status and importance. The beautiful multicolored parrots were very highly valued and were seen to be suitable gifts for one cacique to give to another. The Taíno word for parrots—*guacamayas*—contains the prefix "gua," which also appears in the words for gold (*guanín*, sometimes also called *caona*), in the names of caciques (Guarionex and Guacanagarí), and in the names of some plants.

This was the beginning of a series of encounters with the Taíno caciques of northern Hispaniola. Colón's ship had been on the coast of Hispaniola for ten days, with signal fires continually announcing his presence, yet he had been carefully avoided by the inhabitants of the island. After his emissaries made their trip up the valley of Les Trois Rivièrs and established communication with the cacique there, the situation changed. Although his role was still indistinct at this point, the Admiral appears to have taken

---

[10]For the villages that they had seen until this point, the explorers had always guessed that about twenty people lived in each house. Based on archaeological evidence from Hispaniola, an estimate of 1,000 houses is probably excessive, for 150 *caney*s would have housed 3,000 people. Las Casas's transcription of the *Journal* refers to "la población de 1.000 casas y de más de 3.000 hombres"—a town of 1,000 houses and more than 3,000 *men* (cf. Navarrete's "inhabitants"). Even allowing for some exaggeration, this was certainly the largest village they had seen up to that time.

on an ambiguous position in the Taíno cultural order, having qualities of both a Taíno cacique and a god. Whichever he was, however, he must have seemed a powerful and dangerous presence to the local caciques, a presence which could no longer be ignored but which possibly could be turned into an advantage in the competition for social and political status among caciques.

The first of the visits from local leaders came on Sunday, December 16. In attempting to sail eastward along the north coast of Hispaniola, Colón had spent several days tacking back and forth in the 8-km (5-mi) strait between Hispaniola and the island they called Tortuga (Ile de la Tortue). On one of their several stops at the mouth of Les Trois Rivièrs (present day Port-de-Paix), they were met at the beach by five hundred people and, standing behind them, according to the journal, was their king (Las Casas, *Historia*, I:262; Columbus 1893:112). Many of the people came out to the boats and traded small pieces of gold with the sailors. The king stayed on the shore and watched. From the ship, Colón noted that he was treated with "reverence and respect." Following Las Casas's account,

> The Admiral sent him a present, which they say he received with
> grave dignity, and that he was just a boy of twenty-one years, with
> an old tutor [ayo, which means "tutor" or "teacher"] and other
> councilors who asked questions and answered for him, for he spoke
> very little. One of the Indians that the Admiral had brought talked
> with him, saying that the Christians came from the sky and that
> they were going about looking for gold (although it seemed highly
> incongruous that anyone would come down from heaven to go
> about looking for gold), and that they wanted to go to the island
> of Baneque. The king responded that that was good and that Baneque had a lot of gold. (*Historia*, I:262)

That afternoon, the young cacique and his entourage came out to the *Santa María*. Through his struggling interpreters Colón gave a simplified version of his greetings to the Gran Khan. He tried to explain that he had come to these islands to take possession of them for the most powerful sovereigns in the world. The cacique and his party could not be convinced (because the interpreters could not believe it either) that the foreigners had not come from the sky, and so they assumed the king and queen of Castille were merely other beings who lived there.

Colón ordered that Castillian food be brought for the king.

He took one bite and passed the rest to the people who had come with him. The journal does not record what he was served, but it was probably three-month-old sea bread, or hardtack, and salted meat from Palos, along with Spanish wine. It is difficult to tell whether his indifference to the food was because it was repulsive to him or because he felt that the people accompanying him should have been served as well. Another possibility is that he was disturbed by the way Colón had inadvertently transposed the ritual order of Taíno greeting, in which food is exchanged before gifts. This complex interaction of Castillian and Taíno rituals of feasting and gift giving was very important in structuring the interactions of the two parties during the early contact period.

On the next day some of the explorers went to the nearby village to trade for gold. There they met a person whom the Admiral considered to be the "governor" of the province. Several caciques are mentioned over the course of a few days during this period, and the terminology used to identify them is indistinct. Colón had not used the word "cacique" in the journal until December 16 but had used other words such as "señor" (lord) to reflect the authority of the Taíno leaders. The Spaniards' presence apparently attracted people to the local villages from a distance, so a cacique's presence in a village does not necessarily mean that he lived there. It is not clear whether the "gobernador" the trading party met was the young cacique Colón had met the day before. This cacique had a large leaf-shaped piece of hammered gold and broke off piece after piece, trading them individually to the competing party of Spaniards.

That afternoon, back at the beach near the ships, a fascinating example of the competition for an effective relationship with the Europeans took place.

In the afternoon, a canoe arrived from Tortuga with forty men, and when it arrived at the beach, all of the people of the village, in a sign of peace, sat down on the ground, and most of the people on the canoe began to come in to the land. The aforementioned king [presumably the "gobernador" that had traded the leaf of gold in pieces] arose by himself and, with threatening words, made them get back in, splashing water at them with his hands and throwing stones into the water; that was the extent of his anger. After the advancing group had gone back to their canoe with much obedience and humility, he put a stone in the hand of the Admiral's Alguacil [one of the officers, Diego de Arana] who was next to him, but the

Alguacil did not want to throw it. The king showed there that he favored the Admiral and the Christians; the ones in the canoe returned to Tortuga without any argument. (Las Casas, *Historia*, I:264–65)

The caciques seemed to recognize the value of these strangers as sources of exotic goods and as allies, whether supernatural or human. Yet their reaction to the Spaniards' presence always seemed equivocal. Immediately following the rock-throwing episode at the beach, the cacique said to the Admiral (or so Colón understood) that there was more gold on the island of Tortuga than there was on Hispaniola. Having seen a good deal of the well-populated and cultivated island of Tortuga, Colón did not accept this, believing that Tortuga did not have enough rivers for there to be gold. In his willingness to have Colón leave, however, the cacique on the beach was like the twenty-one-year-old cacique, who, after being greeted by the Admiral, had also been anxious to recommend that the Spaniards go to Babeque to find gold.

December 18 was the Feast of the Annunciation, which the explorers celebrated by dressing the ships with all of their banners and flags. Coincidentally, and to good effect, it was this day that the young cacique returned with two hundred of his followers to visit the Admiral. He arrived seated on a litter carried by four men and was ferried out to the *Santa María* along with a small company of his people. Colón and some of the officers were celebrating the afternoon feast on the deck, shadowed by the poop deck. Las Casas quoted Colón's handwritten journal verbatim.

When the young cacique came aboard the ship he found that we had already begun to eat at the table beneath the castle of the poop deck, and he quickly walked over and sat right next to me; he wouldn't let me come to greet him, nor even get up from the table, but wanted me to continue eating. And when he came beneath the castle, he gave a hand signal that everyone else should stay back, which they all obeyed with the greatest respect in the world, and all of them sat down out on the deck (except for two men of mature age which I guess are his advisors and tutors, who sat at this feet). I thought that he wanted to eat some of our food, and ordered some things be brought. When the food was put before him, he took from each thing a small bite as though he was the food taster, then sent the rest to his people, and all of them ate some. He did the same thing with his drink, only raising it to his mouth then giving it to the others, all with a marvelous dignity and very few words. (*Historia*, I:265–66)

Colón was more astute than he knew when he remarked that the king acted as a food taster ("se toma para hacer la salva"). The young cacique was acting out a role in this context that is remarkably similar to the king's role in a wide range of "chiefdom" or middle-range hierarchical societies known ethnographically and historically. The cacique intercedes between the Taíno world and the chaotic non-Taíno world, as much in the interactions with these dangerous and unpredictable foreigners as with the dangerous and unpredictable Caribbean hurricanes. His food tasting is such an intercession.

The way he received the food, tasted it, and then distributed it on to his subjects also recalls the classic formulations of the redistributional structure of chiefdom societies (Carneiro 1970, 1983; Earle 1977, 1987; Service 1971). On the *Santa María*, the young cacique acts just as he would in a feast for his personal *zemi*, or spirit helper, one of the most important Taíno ceremonies. In that feast, after purifying themselves and singing the songs that commemorate the *zemi*'s great deeds of the past, all the people bring in baskets and baskets of food and lay them at the feet of the cacique. He takes a bite, then gives it all back, and the feast begins. In this act, he expresses his ownership of the food and of the land and labor with which it was produced.

Colón, through the luck of sitting down to eat when he did, kept the Taíno ritual order of chiefly greeting intact—eat first, then exchange gifts.

> After eating, one of the young cacique's attendants brought him a belt[11] that was somewhat like the Castillian ones but of a different workmanship, and he gave it to me, along with two very delicate pieces of worked gold. From these pieces I gathered that they did not have much of it, but that they were not far from where there is a lot. I saw that he was pleased by a drapery [arambel] that was hanging above my bed, and I gave it to him along with some very nice pieces of amber I was wearing around my neck, some red shoes,

---

[11]This belt is perhaps one that is now at the Ethnographic Museum of Vienna. It was probably a gift from Carlos V to one of his German cousins.

and a vial of water flavored with orange blossoms. He was so satisfied by all of this that it was marvelous. It caused him and his tutor and his advisers great pain that they could not understand me, nor I them; Nevertheless, they made it clear to me that if there was anything there that I wanted, the island was at my command. (Las Casas, *Historia*, I:265–66)

Like parrots and parrot feathers, the belt the young cacique gave the admiral had special significance in Taíno culture. The Taíno made quite realistic pottery vessels which often represented individuals sitting on the stools, or *dujo*s, associated with high sociopolitical status and wearing elaborately worked belts. The belts that still exist are laboriously constructed of spun cotton interwoven with objects like small shells (often thousands), pieces of gold, and dog's teeth. In some cases a face presumed to be a principal Taíno god is woven into the front on the belt (Alegría 1980:8–12).

Among the Taíno, especially on Puerto Rico, belts took a second form. These were the intricately carved stone belts that were associated (in both the Caribbean and Mesoamerica) with the ball game. These belts were carved using a pecking technique from a single igneous rock and were enhanced with details to make them look like their organic models. These heavy stone rings were worn around the waist by some of the players on the ceremonial occasions when the ball game was played.

Some time passed after the young cacique had eaten and gifts had been exchanged before the party was ready to leave. Colón sent them ashore in the ships' boats and saluted them by firing the lombards. Once on shore the cacique climbed into his litter and left.

Over the next few days, the competition among local caciques for the explorers' attention was intense. On Friday, December 21, six of the Spaniards were sent to a large village near the bay where they were anchored. They were feted with "all the honor [the villagers] could devise." While they were away on this expedition, more canoes came to the *Santa María*, asking that the Admiral come and meet with their cacique, who was standing on the shore. While engaged with this large group, more emissaries from a third cacique were waiting in canoes with an invitation for Colón to come to another place in a bay, where their cacique was waiting. Colón answered this summons as well, going in the *Santa María*'s

armed boat and never leaving the beach, despite their pleading
for him to come and receive hospitality at their village.

While Colón was away from the *Santa María*, another cacique
and his entourage had arrived by seagoing canoes from the west.
Disappointed by the Admiral's absence and the stampede of other
caciques trying to make contact with the Europeans, he had turned
for home. Colón was disappointed that he had left, however, and
sent a small party in the ship's boat to catch him. All along the
northwest coast of Hispaniola they had been hearing stories of
the fabulous gold-rich islands to the northwest, of which Babeque
was the most often mentioned. Colón thought that he had missed
his chance to see the cacique of that island and to find out whether
there really was gold in abundance there. The party who followed
the canoes found that the cacique was not from the western island
but that his village was inland from the western part of the bay.

The next days were similarly frenzied, as the people of the entire
northeast coast of the island tried to meet with the Europeans,
have them come to their villages, and exchange food and presents.
Colón continued to send out parties to visit the nearby villages,
while he stayed on or near the ships. On the twenty-second he
counted 120 canoes pressed in around the *Santa María* and *Niña*.
He estimated that a thousand people had been on the canoes,
and that another five hundred had swum to the ships. On the
twenty-third the journal records visits from "five caciques, or the
sons of caciques, with all of their houses, women and children,
to see the Christians" (Las Casas, *Historia*, I:274). "The Admiral
knew for certain," Las Casas continued, "that if they held the
Christmas celebration in this port, all of the people in the whole
island would come."

The Spaniards' interest in cassava bread, skeins of cotton, arrows, and parrots had quickly waned; all they wanted to trade
for was gold. Even the relentless trading of trinkets for grains
of gold had become exhausting. The canoes were at the side of
the ship twenty-four hours a day. Colón was determined to push
eastward and find the mine from which the gold came.

On Sunday, December 23, one of the exploring parties was
taken to a village they described as "the largest of the villages
they had seen, with the best-ordered streets and houses; and gathered around the plaza, which was very well swept, was the whole
population of the town—more than two thousand men and infinite women and children; they were all staring at the Christians

rejoicing with the greatest admiration" (p. 274). This village was called *Guarico* and was the seat of *Guacanagarí*, the most important cacique of the northeast part of the island. Colón wanted to visit this village, which was some distance to the southeast, but decided to leave the safety (and onslaught of visitors) of the bay of Santo Tomás (modern Bahía de Acúl) and make the inland march to Guacanagarí's village from one of the ports that lie to the east. He also wanted to follow a number of leads he had received about a source of gold called *Cibao* (which Colón believed to be a corruption of the word "Cipangu").

The Loss of the *Santa María* and the Return to Spain

It was Christmas Eve, and after four difficult days of interaction with the local people, the *Santa María* and *Niña* were at sea again. They were tacking to the east against a light breeze with quartered sails and barely making headway. Their route had been scouted out by one of the ship's boats, and the *Niña* was sailing out ahead of the *Santa María*. About 11 P.M. the watch changed, and as he usually did, Colón left the helm to the master of the ship, Juan de la Cosa, and went to his cabin. Along with most of the crew, he had not slept at all the night before. The excitement of having people coming onto the ship from all directions to see the foreigners had kept them all awake. La Cosa, in turn, gave the tiller to a young ship's boy to hold and fell asleep as well. About midnight the *Santa María* drifted onto a sandbank so gently that no one was even awakened by the contact.

The young pilot might just as well have slammed the ship onto a reef, for the *Santa María* was doomed. Colón had some men launch the ship's boat and haul the anchor out some distance astern so that they could try to winch the ship off the sandbar, but instead they rowed off in pursuit of the *Nina*, about 2 km (1.2 mi) away. The master of the *Niña* would not let them board and sent the boat from his own ship back, but by then it was too late. The current had turned the *Santa María* across the low swell, and the makeshift caulking they had applied in Cuba could not hold out the sea; the ship rocked sideways, then split open.

Colón sent his Alguazil and another of the Spanish nobility in one of the boats to ask the help of the cacique Guacanagarí, whose village was very near where the wreck occurred. The *Niña*, now the only hope of getting back to Spain, could not get close to the wreck without risking the *Santa María's* fate. Martín Alonso Pinzón and the other caravel *Pinta* had not been seen for more than a month. Colón moved to the *Niña* and stood a safe distance offshore for the rest of the night.

Guacanagarí's people came very quickly with a fleet of large canoes and ferried the cargo of the *Santa María* to shore. The Alguazil reported that Guacanagarí wept on hearing the news and periodically through the night sent his relations and lieutenants weeping to the Admiral to console him. The rescue was more effective than anything Colón had hoped for, as the contents of the *Santa María* were quickly shuttled to shore and piled on the beach. The crew's perception was that their already tenuous fate would be sealed if their stores of preserved food were lost, but everything was carried to the village "without a needle missing" (Las Casas, *Historia*, 1:278–79). Guacanagarí cleared out two very large houses in his village for the Spaniards' use.

Colón was reluctant to leave the *Niña*, perhaps out of fear of being deserted, and stayed on board all the next day. The cortege of people anxious to trade soon caught up with the *Niña* and began asking for "chuque chuque cascabeles," the brass bells that the Indians desired the most. On the twenty-sixth Guacanagarí and some of his people came out to the caravel to console the foreigners and offer the most generous hospitality they could. Colón agreed to go to the village and was royally treated. The customary feast was held as soon as they reached the village. Colón gave Guacanagarí a blouse, which among the Spanish was a symbol of high birth and wealth, and gave him a pair of gloves. In return, Colón was given a carved mask, with gold ornaments as eyes and ornamentation, and several other pieces of gold jewelry which symbolized high status, authority, and spiritual power among the Taíno. Over the next few days a genuine and remarkable rapport developed between the two men that would last for several years.

After expressing their recognition of the authority and power of the other, Colón began to try to demonstrate his own superiority. He asked for a Turkish bow that was in his equipment and promptly shot an arrow at one of his men (who had been warned). Guacanagarí's reaction to this curious display apparently satisfied the Admiral. For good measure, however, he had the men fire a bombarda and an espingarda, two weapons that despite their inaccuracy and peril to the person holding them, made a tremendous noise, and Guacanagarí and all of his people fell flat on the ground.

A great believer in predestination, Colón by now accepted that his God had caused the people of Palos to provide him with such an inadequate ship, caused the crew to fall asleep, guided the *Santa María* onto the bank, and brought about all of the events of the last few days so that a settlement would be established at the place he now named Navidad. This situation seemed better each day. Volunteers were anxious to be allowed to stay behind and accumulate a fortune in gold, Guacanagarí appeared to want them to stay, and on December 27, word reached them that the long-lost *Pinta* was anchored in a bay on the north coast.

Thirty-eight men were to stay at Navidad. While consistently recording in his journal that it would not be needed, Colón ordered that a small fort be built from the decks and hull of the *Santa María*, with a large cellar inside. Colón and the *Niña* stayed in the bay before Guacanagarí's village for almost two weeks, building the fortaleza, resupplying the caravel, and deciding what of both ships' cargo would go back to Spain. Colón and his officers met several times with Guacanagarí. One such meeting was remarkable for its image of the political geography of Guacanagarí's part of the island and for the way the two leaders communicated with one another through giving gifts.

> On Sunday, December 30, the Admiral went on shore to eat, arriving at the same time as five kings who were subjects of this great lord Guacanagarí. All had crowns of gold on their heads, representing their great authority. . . . When the Admiral landed, the king came to receive him and took him to the house [that he had given to the Spaniards], where there was a low platform and stools, and he seated the Admiral on one of them with great courtesy and veneration, and then he took the crown off of his head and put it on the Admiral's head. The Admiral took off a necklace of very nice beads [alaqueques] of many pretty colors that looked very nice and put it on Guacanagarí, and he also took off his cape of fine wool that he had worn that day and put it around his shoulders and sent for some colored boots and put them on his feet. He also gave him a large silver ring, because the Admiral knew that the king had seen a sailor with a big ring of silver and would have done much for it; it is true that they think a great deal of things made of white metal, whether it is silver or tin. (Las Casas, *Historia*, I:287–88)

The "coronation" of the Admiral meant a lot more within the European set of cultural categories than it did among the Taíno. Capes of parrot feathers, stools of black wood, finely woven belts, and masks seem to have carried greater symbolic importance, especially with references to political and spiritual power. But to Colón the crown meant a further transference of Guacanagarí's fealty to Colón, and through him, to the sovereigns of Castille. Conversely, receiving the Admiral's cape probably meant a great deal more to Guacanagarí and the caciques with him than Colón knew.

In part because of Colón's vulnerability after the sinking of the *Santa María* and in spite of (or perhaps because of) their almost complete inability to communicate verbally, Guacanagarí and Colón's relationship emerged as one of near-parity and mutual respect and acceptance. In the rest of the brief contact period on Hispaniola, this kind of alliance was almost unknown.

On January 4 Colón and the people who were going with him on the *Niña* finally left Guacanagarí and the thirty-eight men remaining at the little fortress of Navidad. Having heard that Martín Alonso Pinzón was still alive and to the east of him, Colón was anxious to make a course for Spain. He may have been afraid that the Pinzón family would try to take credit for the major part of the discoveries of the first voyage and lay claim to the Colón family's privileges (which, in fact, they did [Floyd 1973]). Colón left almost all the trade goods with Diego de Arana, Pero Gutiérrez, and Rodrigo de Escobedo, the men in charge of Navidad. He hoped that by the time of this return voyage they would have turned it into a fortune in gold.

The *Niña* could sail into the wind more effectively than the *Santa María* ever could, and they made good progress over the next few days. They met up with the *Pinta* on January 6 near Montecristi. The rendezvous was a hostile one for both parties. Colón charged Pinzón with desertion, saying that through his greed and bad judgment he had threatened everyone's survival by leaving the *Santa María* and *Niña*. Colón pointed out (very likely repeatedly) that he was the Admiral of the Ocean Sea, he was in charge of the expedition, and Pinzón was under his orders. All of this was true, but it was highly impolitic to say so quite so directly. Most of the crew of both ships were from Palos and were probably overjoyed to find their friends and relatives on the *Pinta* still alive. Vicente Yáñez Pinzón was the master of the *Niña* and, along with most of both crews, was not pleased to see his brother abused by this self-important and intensely hierarchical Genoese.

The greatest disappointment, resulting in part from the Pinzón-Colón feud, is that there is no detailed historical account of the month the *Pinta* spent apart from the rest of the expedition. In his journal, which was his report to the king and queen, Colón is absorbed with condemning Pinzón's actions and refuting his excuses. He mentions only in passing that the *Pinta* had visited Babeque and had found no gold, had anchored in the same cove in front of Navidad, and had received information about the other large islands of *Yamaye* (Jamaica) and *Boriquén*, (Puerto Rico). Pinzón also penetrated some distance into the interior of Hispaniola and met with some of the caciques that would figure so prominently in the events of the next few years. It was in Colón's interest, however, to demonstrate that Pinzón had not discovered anything new and had no legal claim on the potential profits. In subsequent years, the Pinzón family sued the Colón family (unsuccessfully) for part of their spoils in the exploitation of Hispaniola, but the minute details of Martín Alonso Pinzón's interactions with the Indians he had met were lost forever.

This chill between Pinzón and Colón affected the rest of the voyage. They made as much speed as they could eastward along the north coast of Hispaniola and had only one major incident with the inhabitants of the island. On the Samaná peninsula, the northeasternmost tip of land on Hispaniola, they met a group of people who looked and spoke differently from those they had met in the west. When they stopped to take on water and food, the landing party met a group of men carrying large bows and arrows. They managed to talk with them and trade for some of the bows and arrows. One of the Indians agreed to come and meet the Admiral. Las Casas reproduces Colón's description.

> He had a very strange looking face, totally darkened with charcoal (but it was not really charcoal, but instead a kind of ink made from a plant), although in all of these parts they paint themselves in diverse colors; these ones wear their hair very long, gathered up and bundled into a hairnet made of parrot feathers, and he was completely naked. The Admiral suspected that he was a Carib of those who ate people, but he was not, and they never found any who did that on this island. . . .
>
> They asked where the Caribs were, and he showed them that they

were to the east; they asked him about gold, and he also pointed east to the island of San Juan [Puerto Rico], which the Admiral had seen the day before they rounded the entrance to this bay. (*Historia,* I:303).

When asking him about gold, Colón must have realized that although the Indian understood much of what they said, the people of Samaná had different words for many things. Colón gave him some of the remaining trade goods and sent him back to shore.

A larger group of Indians armed with bows and clubs were on shore waiting, and the envoy showed them the trade goods and told them not to be alarmed by the foreigners. Some of the men in the landing party began to trade for more of the bows, but after the Indians had given up two they became very nervous. A fight broke out, and the Spaniards retaliated with swords and crossbows. The battle apparently lasted only a few seconds, as both groups were in full retreat. The next day a reconciliation was made when a cacique came out to the caravel to exchange food and presents.

On January 16, just under one hundred days since they landed at San Salvador, the two caravels (both leaking alarmingly) caught a favorable wind and steered for Spain.

3

✳✳✳✳✳✳

The Vega Real

In the years 1494 to 1498 a conjunction of events brought about the destruction of the indigenous sociopolitical system of Hispaniola. During this period there was dissention and warfare among factions of the Spanish forces, coupled with despair of adequate support or assistance from Spain. Anticipated profits from the goldfields did not materialize. For many of the conquistadores the only way to survive was to move constantly from Indian village to village. This was, for both Spanish and Taíno, the darkest time of the contact period.

The focal point for many of the events leading to the collapse of the Taíno was the island's large interior valley, the Vega Real. There were two abortive skirmishes in the Vega—in November 1494 and March 1495. In 1495 and 1496 there was extensive famine and plague among the Indians. In July of 1497 the remaining caciques formed an unsuccessful coalition against the Spanish. The final event discussed in this chapter is the flight of one of the principal caciques of the region, Guarionex, from the Vega Real.

The documentary coverage of these four years is uneven. The initial fascination with the Indians in journals and letters gradually abated; the political and military intrigues by the pro- and anti-Colón alliances absorbed most of the interest of the chroniclers. The accounts of the events in this four-year span of time nevertheless allow a partial reconstruction of several aspects of the Taíno sociopolitical system. The events described in this chapter yield insight into the political, economic, and social structure of Taíno society.

First, the collective diplomatic and military activities undertaken by groups of caciques in the Vega Real informs a discussion of the existence and operation of confederacies among the Taíno. The meaning of these rather ephemeral alliances is somewhat difficult to assess because of the extraordinary presence of the aggressive Spanish forces.

Second, the famine of 1495 and 1496 suggests some of the vulnerabilities of the Taíno system of intensive agricultural production. Other factors, especially disease, certainly were involved in this crisis period, but the famine period provides a narrative context in which to discuss the *conuco* mode of intensified agriculture and its importance for the complex societies of Hispaniola.

Finally, the events in the Vega Real offer evidence for the presence of several interacting ethnic groups on Hispaniola at the time of contact. There seem to have been linguistic and cultural diversity even across short distances.

The Entrada of Colón and Founding of Santo Tomás

Returning to Hispaniola on his second voyage in November of 1493, Colón and his company found the colony at Navidad in ruins and all of its European occupants dead. Instead of attacking the probable participants in the fort's destruction, Colón accepted Guacanagarí's story that other powerful caciques on the island had destroyed the settlement. This was expedient, since the Spaniard's stores were already low and Guacanagarí was happy to provide food. Colón's decision also kept an uneasy peace on the island for another year.

Besides the supply of native food Guacanagarí provided, there was not much to recommend the site of Navidad. Its location, after all, had been selected by the shipwreck of the Santa María the year before. The success of the first voyage had provided Colón with the backing to bring a fleet of seventeen vessels, and some of these caravels scouted the north coast for a new settlement site. They found a suitable location 160 km (100 mi) to the east, overlooking the mouth of the Río Bajabonico. Here, the port of Isabela was founded.

The doctor Chanca, a physician on the voyage, described the place.

> The land is very rich in all things; It is next to a large river and another of reasonable size, with remarkably good water: A town called Marta [later Isabela] was built on the banks between the river in

such a way that it was protected by the river and a barricade of cliffs, so that on that side no other fortification is needed; the other side is enclosed by a grove of trees so thick that a rabbit could not get through it, and so green that it could not ever burn. They have started to dredge a channel in the river, which the builders say will come into the middle of the settlement, and along which grist and sawmills can be located, driven by the water. Many gardens have been made, and it is certain that they will produce more in eight days than could be grown in twenty in Spain. Many Indians arrive continually with their caciques, which are like their *capitanes*, and many women. All are bringing loads of *ages*, sort of like turnips and a very good food, which we have cooked in every way imaginable. (Chanca 1932:60–61)

These Indian visitors were questioned closely about the sources of gold on the island. The general answer was that there were two, one called *Niti*, in the province of the cacique Caonabo, and the second and greater was called *Cibao*. Colón had intended to forestall the search for the goldfields until Isabela was established and a report had been sent to Castille. Although they had been on Hispaniola for only a little more than a month, many of the Spaniards were suffering from illness and the strange diet. According to Chanca's reports, one-third of the company had fallen sick in the space of a few days at Isabela (p. 62).

Nevertheless, the attraction of *Niti* and *Cibao* was irresistible. Two scouting parties were sent out with guides to see these areas. One group, led by Alonso de Hojeda, crossed the northern cordillera into the valley of the Vega Real and continued southward to the edge of the great Cordillera Central (figure 6). As was common in the early years of exploration, the only gold they accumulated was given as gifts from the local Indians, who had learned quickly that the only material gifts appreciated by the strangers were gold and food (with the exception, in the early years, of the iguana).

Hojeda and his company were gone fourteen days and returned on January 20, 1494. They reported that "they found gold in so many places a man could not name them all—that in truth they had found more than fifty streams and rivers that contained gold" (pp. 66–67). With this, the desire to march en masse to the interior overcame even Colón, an explorer not much given to leaving the sight of his ships.

The second party penetrated farther south into the Cordillera

Figure 6. Central Hispaniola, with the location of early Spanish forts

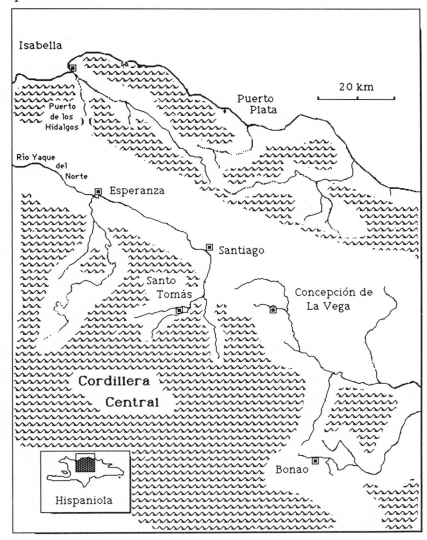

Central. By their telling they had almost reached the territory of the cacique called Caonabo. They had probably continued up into the headwaters of the Río Yaque del Norte, near the future site of Santo Tomás. Since they returned to Isabela only a day after Hojeda, it is unlikely that they penetrated much farther. Neither group had encountered hostility or resistance from the Indians, and in fact both had been helped and fed continually by a succession of caciques.

Despite the elation brought by the promise of imminent wealth in the interior, the month of February 1494, was spent fighting for the survival of the large company camped at Isabela. Over half were sick, and the remaining rations of European food—sea biscuits and wine, by this point—were almost gone. Colón sent twelve of his seventeen ships back to Spain under Antonio de Torres with more samples of gold and Caribbean artifacts (including sixty parrots and twenty-six captives abducted in the Lesser Antilles). Colón also sent a memorandum to the crown reporting on the fate of Navidad and of their progress to date. He asked for three caravels of supplies, especially food, clothes, and arms.

On March 12, Colón led his army into the northern cordillera. A few were left with the ships at Isabela, and the large and by all accounts impressive company followed the route of Hojeda. "Because the roads that the Indians used were no wider than what we would call paths [sendas], and since they were not encumbered with equipment or clothes and did not have carts," the Admiral ordered some men to go ahead and clear a road (Las Casas, *Historia*, I:368).

Colón intended to make a great impression on the Taíno and thus marched in military formation behind armored cavalry and banners. He had his men fire guns and give trumpet fanfares whenever they came upon new groups of people. Many of the Indians who had congregated around Isabela followed the army into the interior, and so the entire company was perhaps four or five hundred people. Reaching a vantage overlooking Hispaniola's immense inland valley, by far the largest and richest area of its kind in the Antilles, the army was greatly impressed.

> Reaching the summit at the Puerto de los Hidalgos, they saw the great plain, a thing which I think (and I do not think that I exaggerate) is one of the most admirable things in the world, more impressive and worthy than the mundane and temporal things of the world. . . . It is eighty leagues long and twenty or thirty leagues

from one side to the other [approx. 240 km (150 mi) long and 48 km (30 mi) wide], from the mountains where the Admiral and his people were; the view from there was so green, so unspoiled, so colorful, all so full of beauty, that it appeared to them that they had reached a part of heaven. (P. 368)

Down on the plain, Las Casas continues, they "passed many villages and were received as though they had come from the sky" (p. 368). Ferdinand Colón writes, "In the course of the journey they passed many Indian towns, consisting of round thatched houses, with such small doors that it requires a person entering to stoop very low" (Columbus 1824:108–9).

The behavior of the Indians that had accompanied the party from Isabela was remarkable to the Spaniards.

> [As soon as] they entered any of those houses they took what they liked best, and yet the owners seemed not to be at all displeased, as if all things were in common among them. In like manner the people of the country were disposed to take from the Christians whatever they thought fit, thinking our things had been in common like theirs; but they were soon undeceived. (P. 109)

The political affiliations and geographic origins of the Indians escorting the Admiral are unclear. Some may have come from the area around Isabela or the nearby mountain valleys. Some seem to have come from the cacicazgo of Guacanagarí, near the site of Navidad. Guacanagarí had allied himself with the Colón family during the first voyage and continued in that role for ten years. His people would fight on the side of the Spaniards in the battles that were to come in the Vega Real, and most important, they acted as spies as the Europeans became acclimated to the political environment of the island. It is likely that Guacanagarí's alliance with the Colón family was calculated to raise his stature in the hierarchy of caciques on Hispaniola. Sauer (1966) has suggested, and I agree, that Guacanagarí was subordinate to another more powerful cacique; through his association with Colón and the Admiral's army, he seems to have raised his sociopolitical status considerably. In doing so at the beginning, Guacanagarí may have put himself in a position in which he had no choice but to ally himself with the Colóns for protection. He had thrown the blame for the destruction of Navidad onto other caciques, including Caonabo, and had brought about that cacique's destruction.

The behavior of the Indians who took things from the Vega

Real villages is interesting and somewhat difficult to understand. It may be that this conduct was generally appropriate or that it legitimated social ties between the Indians in Colón's company and those in the Vega Real villages. In this case, appropriation of goods would be the right of the guest or kinsman, or else possessions were in fact held in common, as the chroniclers assumed. Alternately, appropriation may have been an acceptable action for Indian conquerors, even though there had been no battle. The former interpretation may be supported by the Indians' attempts to take things in turn from the Spaniards' equipment. In other situations, however, particularly among the Taíno elite, emphasis was placed on elaborate gift-giving ceremonies, not on gift taking. This may qualify the former interpretation, in which goods were taken without ceremony.

Another incident reflecting the Taíno sense of material possession occurred during Colón's first entrada. The army crossed the Río Yaque del Norte with the help of Indian canoes and porters and traveled southeastward in the foothills of the Cordillera Central. They crossed another river, which they called the River of Gold (the Río Bao, south of modern Santiago, figure 6). After this crossing they came into a large village,

> from which most of the people fled, hiding in the closest mountains as soon as they saw the Spaniards coming; the rest of the people remained in the village and hid in their thatch houses and in their total simplicity barred the doors with a bundle of grass, as though you could not push the wall in with a little effort. . . . What stronger argument could there be of their innocence and simplicity? (Las Casas, *Historia*, I:369–70)

Ferdinand Colón says that "according to their customs, no one dares to break in at a door that is barred up in this manner, as they have no wooden doors or any other means of shutting up their houses" (Columbus 1824:109).

Villages became larger and more frequent as Colón moved from west to east along the borders of the Vega Real. Crossing the watershed between the westward-flowing Yaque drainage and the eastward-flowing Yuna, he came upon a small river which he called the Río Verde. On March 15, 1494, the company walked down the banks of the Río Verde, passing several large villages. The area would soon be the focal point for the conflict between the Indians and Spanish. A year later the Admiral's brother Barto-

lomé would build the most important of the inland fortalezas—
Concepción de la Vega—in the valley of the Río Verde (figure
6). The villages they passed were subject to the cacique Guarionex,
a principal figure in the conflicts to come.

Then as now, the area around the Río Verde was one of the
most densely populated in the valley. In the 1950 census, the population density in the area around Concepción de la Vega was
63.7 people per km^2 almost three times the density of the area
where Colón had first entered the Vega Real. No archaeological
survey has been done in the Vega Real, and attempting to reconstruct the demographic characteristics of the island from the ethnohistoric documents has proven extremely problematic. Even the
most general parameters are elusive: Cook and Borah (1971:408)
have estimated that there were as many as eight million people
on the island in 1492. Representative of the other extreme, Rosenblat (1976:59) estimates that there were about only one hundred
thousand people.

The gradient in population density today and, by inference, before the arrival of the Spaniards is in part a reflection of the rainfall
patterns across the Vega Real. In the western Vega, where Colón
crossed, the present annual rainfall is about 790 mm (31 in; rainfall figures are from Fuente García 1976:164–68); in the eastern
part of the valley, at modern Villa Riva, annual rainfall is 2,255
mm (89 in). In the drainage of the Río Verde there are about
1,400 mm (55 in) of rainfall per year. In the west, furthermore,
the dry season from December to March is more marked than
in the east, with less than 50 mm (2 in) per month during the
dry months. The island, and particularly the areas under intensive
cultivation like the Vega Real, has probably experienced significant
ecological change over the past five hundred years, but it is possible to assume that proportionally, pre-Columbian population and
rainfall figures paralleled the modern figures.

Before heading into the mountains, Colón sent a party of men
and mules back to Isabela for bread and wine. It was a round
trip of 160 km (100 mi) and probably took a week to accomplish.
Unfortunately, neither Ferdinand Colón nor Las Casas specify
where the company stayed. Later incidents support the conjecture
that it was in the valley of the Río Verde, within the cacicazgo
of Guarionex. The deference shown Guarionex by the Colón family in the events to come may indicate that they were his guests
for a week. One of the Admiral's priorities thereafter was to establish a fortaleza very close to the village of Guarionex.

On the return of the pack train, the company headed into the land of Cibao,

> a very rough land, of large and very high mountain ranges, covered by rocks large and small; it was thus well named by the Indians Cibao, from *ciba*, which means stone or rock pile—the land of many rocks. Among the stones there was a short grass, which did not even cover the rocks. . . . The province contained infinite rivers and streams, in all of which gold was found. (Las Casas, *Historia*, I:371)

Despite their complaints and difficulties with the horses and equipment, the entrada came via a relatively easy route into the rugged Cordillera Central, whose peaks reach 3,087 m (10,128 ft). They collected a substantial amount of gold, almost all volunteered as gifts from the Indians. These gifts were accepted without dismay by the Spaniards. "As Ojeda had travelled before into this country, the Indians had some knowledge of the Christians; and understanding that they came in search of gold, the natives came to meet the admiral everywhere during the march with small quantities of gold which they had gathered, and bringing presents of provisions" (Columbus 1824:110). Perceiving that they were in the heart of the gold-producing area, Colón had a fortaleza of pounded earth and wood built in the narrow valley of the Río Janico. He called it Santo Tomás.

The army returned northward, leaving a garrison under Mosén Pedro Margarite at the fortaleza. The bread and wine Colón had ordered was exhausted or left with the garrison, and there were complaints on the eight-day march to Isabela.

Colón returned to find an epidemic at Isabela; several had died, and most of the remainder were sick. The doctor Chanca and Colón blamed the diseases on the strange diet and humid conditions, but many of the hidalgos who had been conscripted as builders blamed it on overwork. Dissention against the Colón family— always present—was growing and would be a dominant fact in the first two decades of the Spanish occupation of Hispaniola.

The First Skirmishes

The relationship between the Indians and the Spaniards deteriorated very quickly following Colón's entrada. Two days after returning to Isabela, Colón received word that the fort at Santo

Tomás was about to be attacked by the forces of the cacique Caonabo. Seventy men were immediately sent back. The situation at Isabela was becoming worse daily: provisions from Spain were nearly exhausted, and there was an army of Spaniards to be fed.

Needing to reduce the pressure on the fort, Colón sent four hundred men, the majority of the force, into the interior with Alonso de Hojeda, with orders to "march around the country in various directions to strike terror into the Indians, to accustom them to subjection and to enure the Spaniards to the food of the country" (Columbus 1824:113). Hojeda went to Santo Tomás and passed this brief on to Marguerite, taking the post at Santo Tomás for himself. Marguerite, to the irritation of the Colón contingent, "went with all his men to the great plain called Vega Real, or the Royal Plain, ten leagues from Isabela, where he remained without ever endeavouring to traverse and reduce the island" (p. 127).

A series of hostile events followed. Hojeda, while marching to Santo Tomás, ran into trouble at the crossing of the Río Yaque del Norte. Five Indians were acting as porters for three Spaniards who were crossing the river. Instead of ferrying the soldier's clothes across, they turned around in midstream and took the clothes back to their village, leaving the Spaniards naked on the opposite bank. Hojeda reacted violently, capturing the cacique of their village along with two of his kinsmen. He had the ears cut off of one of the cacique's people in the village's plaza and sent the cacique and some of his family back to Isabela in chains— Hojeda had taken seriously the Admiral's order to terrorize the countryside. Another cacique who lived nearby (between Esperanza and Santiago on figure 6) came to Isabela to ask for the prisoner's release. Colón publicly sentenced them to die for their complicity in the theft in order to demonstrate his resolve—and then reprieved them to show his magnanimity.

While this was happening at Isabela, five Spaniards were taken prisoner in the village of the captured cacique. They were rescued by a single horseman, who capitalized on the terror the horse inspired.

The Admiral, wanting to add to his discoveries and to escape the difficult situation on Hispaniola, sailed with three ships to explore the coasts of Jamaica and Cuba. Discipline eroded more quickly under an unpopular council of five he appointed to rule in his absence. Martyr, possibly biased by his long-standing support for the Colón family, notes:

It is a fact that the people who accompanied the Admiral in his second voyage were for the most part undisciplined, unscrupulous vagabonds, who only employed their ingenuity in gratifying their appetites. Incapable of moderation in their acts of injustice, they carried off the women of the islanders under the very eyes of their brothers and their husbands; given over to violence and thieving, they had profoundly vexed the natives.

He adds, however, that the violence was not one-sided. "It had happened in many places that when our men were surprised by the natives, the latter strangled them, and offered them as sacrifices to their gods" (Martyr 1970:106). Herrera (*Historia*, vol. I, chap. 16) reports that around this time a cacique called Juatinango, reputedly a subordinate cacique to Guarionex, captured and killed ten soldiers and then burned a house with forty sick Spaniards inside.

The Capture of Caonabo

The Indian caciques were further incited by the capture of Caonabo, one of the principal caciques of the island. It was the Spaniard's perception, shared by all those recording these incidents, that Caonabo was the most militant and dangerous of the Indian leaders on Hispaniola. Through Guacanagarí's artifice Caonabo had taken most of the blame for the massacre at Navidad, and it was believed that the threat to Santo Tomás came from him as well. This assumption, which was probably at least partially correct, demonstrates the mobility of Caonabo's forces on the island. It is 80 km (50 mi) by air from Corrales de los Indios in San Juan de la Maguana, the archaeological site where Caonabo probably lived. By land through the steep valleys of the Cordillera Central, it was at the minimum 110 difficult kilometers (68 mi)—a journey of about four days.

Nevertheless, dealing with Caonabo became a priority for the Spaniards. Alonso de Hojeda was sent south across the cordillera to the village of Caonabo and later returned with the cacique as a captive. There are several versions of the story of Caonabo's capture, none completely convincing. Martyr says that Caonabo was coming to greet the Admiral with a company of his armed guard. "The consciousness of his crimes disturbed him," Martyr supposes, "for he had cut off the heads of twenty of our men whom he had surprised" (Martyr 1970:107). Caonabo may have been raising a military force to destroy either the blockhouse at Santo Tomás or Isabela itself. Martyr says that it was Colón who actually captured Caonabo, once he had been escorted to Isabela by Hojeda.

The version of the story given by Las Casas has the character of an embellished legend of heroic deeds that might have been told later in the conquest period. This was an important story during the conquest period, one repeated in other chronicles and documents. The battles fought with the Indians on Hispaniola were such routs that even the exaggerated tales of a few men against thousands did not take on heroic qualities. Caonabo, however, had been constructed as a villain in absentia by Colón and others, and thus Las Casas's story of a bloodless defeat by a cunning trick took on added importance.

> By chance, a little before that which I have told, Alonso de Hojeda, of whom . . . I have spoken . . . was sent on a secret mission by the Admiral, by himself with nine Christians, to visit the king Caonabo, who, I have mentioned above, was a very powerful leader and the strongest of all the other leaders on this island; Hojeda was to ask him to come and visit Isabela, and if possible, to capture him with a prearranged trick. . . .
>
> The trick went like this: the Indians called our brass *turey* (and also the other metals that we had brought from Castilla), for the value they placed on things that came from "the sky," because *turey* meant "from the sky," and these things were like their jewels, especially brass. For this reason Alonso de Hojeda took along some manacles and handcuffs that were very well made, subtle and thin and highly polished, and was to give them as a present sent from the Admiral, saying that it was *turey* from Vizcaya,[1] which was meant to mean a very precious thing which came from the sky. Hojeda arrived at the lands and village of the king Caonabo, which they called *Maguana*, which would be sixty or seventy leagues from Isabela, and rode in on his horse and terrified all of the Indians that they saw, because at first the Indians thought that the man and the horse were all one animal. Hojeda said to Caonabo that they had been sent by

---

[1]Biscay, a mining region in Spain and France; taking iron to Vizcaya is the same as taking coals to Newcastle.

the Admiral, the *Guamiquina* of the Christians, which means the leader or "him who is above all the Christians," and that they brought him a present, which they called the *turey* of Vizcaya. Hearing that they had brought *turey*, Caonabo cheered up a great deal, mostly because he had heard of a brass bell that was at the chapel at Isabela, and the Indians who had seen it said that the Christians had a *turey* that could talk, thinking that when a mass was said and all the Christians were pleased by the sound of it because they could understand what it said, and therefore he wanted very much to see it. . . .

. . . and Hojeda went in where Caonabo was; and they say that Hojeda went down on his knees and kissed Caonabo's hands, and said to his companions, "Do as I do." Hojeda said that he had brought him *turey* de Vizcaya and showed him the manacles and handcuffs all polished like silver, and with gestures and some words which Hojeda had already learned, told him that this *turey* had come from the sky and had a great and secret power and that the *Guamiquina* or kings of Castilla put them on like jewels when they did their *areyto*s, which were dances, and they then begged Caonabo to come to the river to rest and wash, which was something widely done. . . .

Caonabo decided to go to the river for the day, and went with some members of his household and a few other people to the river, completely relaxed and without fear, thinking that nine or ten Christians would not be able to do any harm, here in the middle of his land where he had so much power and vassals. After having bathed and rested, Caonabo wanted very badly to have his present of *turey* de Vizcaya and try out its powers, and so Hojeda took Caonabo aside from those that had followed, and put him up on his horse and mounted behind him, and there he snapped shut the handcuffs (which pleased the Christians) and made one or two galloping passes by where the other group was in order to scare them, and the nine Christians came with him on the road to Isabela, acting like they would go a little ways and then return, but little by little they distanced themselves from the watching Indians, who always fled from the horses. . . .

They left with all the speed they could from there along the rough trails, through the mountains, away from them, until after a great deal of work, danger, and hunger, they arrived at Isabela and handed Caonabo over to the Admiral. In this manner and with this campaign, and by the trick of the *turey* of Vizcaya, Alonso de Hojeda captured the great king Caonabo, one of the five principal kings of the island, and thereafter Hojeda was very famous. (*Historia*, I:406–7)

It is difficult to say how much truth there is in the story of the *turey* of Vizcaya. The ruse, however, shows a real sensitivity to the ways in which sociopolitical power was expressed symbolically among the Taíno. Not only did Hojeda offer a gift, he presented it as a cosmically powerful *turey* object. He did not hand it over but moved that they go to the river to bathe, a critical element in the Taíno ceremonies which provided coherence among the Taíno elite (Alegría 1978; Arrom 1975; García Arévalo 1983; López-Baralt 1976). He was able—apparently by design—to frame his gift within the same category as *zemi*s, powerful objects which symbolized the caciques' intimate relationship with cosmic forces—gods in the Catholics' cosmogony.

The doctor Chanca had already observed the phenomenon of *turey* objects on the second voyage.

> In truth they were idolaters, for in their houses they have many
> kinds of figures. When asked what such a figure was, they would
> reply that it is a of *turey*, by which they meant "of the sky." I made
> a pretense of throwing them on the fire, which grieved them so that
> they began to weep. They believe that everything we bring comes
> from heaven and therefore call it *turey*. (Chanca 1847:64)

Some such objects were necessary in the Taíno ritual associated with agricultural production. Ritually invested objects were taken and buried in the fields. This caused substantial confusion when Christian idols were treated in a similar fashion. The Jeronomite friar Ramón Pané, who as a missionary developed perhaps the best understanding of the Taíno ritual of any of the oberservers, chronicles a parody of this behavior in the Vega Real.

> Six men went into the house of prayer which the aforesaid catechu-
> mens who were seven in number had charge of, and by order of
> Guarionex told them that they should take those images which the
> Friar Ramón [Pané himself] had left the custody of the catechumens,
> and rend them and break them. . . . They threw the images down
> on the ground and covered them and made water on them saying
> "Now your fruits will be good and great." And this because they
> buried them in a tilled field saying the fruit would be good which
> was planted there, and all this in mockery. (Quoted in Bourne 1906:30)

A subset of *turey* objects were the more powerfully charged *zemi*s, material objects that had names, personalities, and idiosyncrasies. Primarily, they took the form of triangular, elaborately carved stones, but anthropomorphic images like dolls made of cotton fiber, and a range of other manifestations were also used.

The *zemi*s were not so much the property or symbolized power of a cacique as they were supernatural allies to be venerated and courted. The caciques kept counsel with their respective *zemi*s primarily through the *cohoba* rituals; *cohoba* was a narcotic snuff which produced hallucinogenic trances within which a cacique communicated with supernatural beings.

The rites associated with the *zemi* cults were extremely important in the ritual calendar. They were also a mechanism for the symbolic redistribution of food by the cacique. Benzioni describes a *zemi* ritual.

> When the cacique of *La Española* wished to celebrate a feast in honour of his principal false deity, he commanded all his vassals, both men and women, to come to him on a certain day, and on arrival at the appointed spot, they ranged themselves in order. The cacique then advanced, and entered the temple where the ministers were dressing the idol. There he sat down, playing on a drum, and all the other people followed; first the men, painted black, red and yellow, with plumes of parrots and other feathers, with ornaments of seashells round their necks, their legs, and their arms. The women were not painted at all; the girls were quite naked; the married women had a covering hanging from their waist. . . . Thus they entered the temple, dancing and singing certain of their songs in praise of their idol, while their chief saluted them with his drum. Then, by putting a stick down their throat, they vomited, so that the idol might see that they had nothing bad either in their stomach or their breast. After performing these foolish ceremonies, they all sat down on their heels, and, with a melancholy noise, they sang some more songs. Then some other women entered the temple with baskets adorned with roses and flowers, and filled with bread, and they went round to those who were singing, and repeated a little prayer to them. The singers jumped on their feet to answer, and when they had finished these songs, they began others to the honour and glory of their chief; after which they presented the bread to their idol. The ministers now took and blessed it, and shared it with all the people, as if it was a holy thing or good relic. (Benzioni 1857:79–80)

Gomara (1932:67–68) offers a nearly identical description of the rite, adding that the people save a bit of the redistributed bread through the year "and take as a misfortune the household that is without it, for they are subject to great danger."

Whether the tale of the black *turey* of Viscaya is true in its details or not, it demonstrates that either at the time the events took place or in the writing of the chronicles, a rather sophisticated understanding of some of the Taíno concepts of cosmology and power did exist. The story was probably notable and repeated because an accurate understanding of Taíno culture was skillfully twisted into an effective ruse.

The First Battle of the Vega Real

The events of 1494 and early 1495 ultimately precipitated a collective and violent reaction from Indians in the western Vega. Colón took this as an opportunity to subjugate the island brutally and to establish a tribute system through which gold and food could be collected from the Indians in greater quantity.

At this time, however, the Spaniards had a very poor understanding of the indigenous political geography of the island. Probably only Hojeda and Marguerite, who left no accounts, had a clear idea of the extent, operation, and leadership of the cacicazgos in the Vega Real.

Some of the accounts, especially that of Ferdinand Colón (Columbus 1824), are presented as a military history designed to show the Admiral in a favorable light. In fact, this period was an unrelenting series of defeats for the Indians, especially of the Vega, whose methods of waging war were absolutely ineffective against the Spaniards. Within the accounts of this time, however, are some data on the important caciques and their area of control.

Ferdinand's account begins as follows: "Having resolved to make war upon the refractory natives, he set out from Isabela on the 24th of March 1495, taking Guacanagarí along with him; yet the enterprize seemed difficult, as the malcontent Indians had collected a force of above 100,000 men, whereas the admiral had only about 200 infantry, 20 horsemen, and about the same number of dogs" (Columbus 1824:128). It is certain that this force of 100,000 men, in fact some fraction of that number, represents a collection of people from a number of chiefdoms. Morison (1942:488) believes that they were led by the cacique Guatiguaná. This name had appeared earlier, when he was captured, taken to Isabela, but then escaped before his execution. Las Casas mentions him in connection with his captivity at Isabela, (*Historia*, I:414–15), as does Ferdinand, who says that he was the cacique of *Magdalen* and had killed ten Spaniards (1824:127).

Other political participants in this collective action are the notorious and nameless brothers of Caonabo. They are mentioned only as being dangerous presences around Santo Tomás and in the western Vega Real. Two other caciques—from the fords of the Río Yaque del Norte at Pontón—had been mentioned in connection with the clothes-stealing incident; one had been sentenced to die and reprieved, and the other had pled for his release. Their villages were within 24 km (15 mi) of the site of the battle, but their names are not mentioned.

The cacique Guarionex, who consistently is considered by all of the chroniclers to have been the most powerful cacique in the Vega, is not mentioned at all and seems not to have been involved. As the subjugation of the island continued, Guarionex was a central figure in the negotiations about tribute.

The battle itself was such a rout that Martyr does not even mention it. Ferdinand's description, typical of many other accounts of battles during the period, continues:

> Being well acquainted with the nature and qualities of the Indians, when he was two days' march from Isabela, the admiral divided his small force giving half to his brother the lieutenant [Bartolomé, who had just arrived on the island for the first time], that he might attack the multitude which was scattered over the plain in two places at once, believing that the terror of the noise in two places would throw them into disorder, and put them to flight the sooner, as it actually proved in the event. The battalions of foot fell upon the disordered multitude of the Indians, and broke them with the first discharge of their cross-bows and muskets; the cavalry and the dogs next fell upon them in the most furious manner that they might have no time to rally and the faint-hearted natives fled on every side. (Columbus 1824:128–29)

Many of the natives, men and women, were taken back to Isabela as slaves. Colón remained convinced (despite uneasy hints to the contrary in his most recent letter from the king and queen [Colección de documentos inéditos]) that slaves were going to be the most profitable commodity from Hispaniola in the early years. Many of the Indian leaders were executed, although their number and identity are not mentioned.

The effects of the defeat of this large coalition of Taíno forces are uncertain. With the capture of Caonabo and the possible capture or death of some of his brothers in the first battle in the

Vega Real, the political situation in the cacicazgo of *Maguana* must have been very unsettled. Yet Behecchio, a neighboring cacique from *Xaraguá*, apparently did not try to annex the area until eighteen months later (as discussed in chapter 4).

Guarionex's position in later confederacies seems to have been enhanced by the first battle of the Vega Real. The Spaniards certainly saw him thereafter as the most powerful Indian leader in the valley. Their assessment of Guarionex's importance is evident in the role he had in the discussions of tribute from the Vega Real and the Cibao and in the founding of Concepción de La Vega (the principal inland fortaleza) right next to his village on the Río Verde.

The Tribute System and the Famine of 1495–96

The first battle of the Vega Real occurred in late March 1495. The next major organized rebellion, more desperate and even less successful than the first, did not occur until around June 1497. In the intervening period the population of the Indians on the island was in its steepest decline of the thirty-year period which saw the extinction of the Taíno of Hispaniola.

Cook and Borah have undertaken an extensive reevaluation of the documentary evidence for the population decline, and in their analysis have produced an estimate of "the coefficient of population movement, or the average annual rate of change" (1971:404). For 1496–97 they calculate that the annual rate of decline was -44.20 percent, and for subsequent years a similarly sharp decline (see table).

Cook and Borah's population estimates of the island have been contested by Rosenblat (1976), who would start with a much

Year	Annual Rate of Change (%)	Estimated Population
1496	-44.20	3,770,000
1497	-41.50	2,103,660
1498	-34.39	1,230,641
1499	-34.70	807,429
1500	—	527,251

Source: Adapted from Cook and Borah 1971:401–5

lower initial population figure, but it is likely that their assessment of the catastrophic *rate* of demographic decline is not far from correct (cf. Henige 1978a for a contrasting view). If these figures are accurate, the Indian population of Hispaniola in 1500 would have been only 14 percent of its 1496 level. More than eight of every ten would have died.

The problem of the widely divergent estimates of the population of Hispaniola has been reviewed by Henige (1978a, 1978b) and Zambardino (1978). Both (along with Cook and Borah) acknowledge the difficulty in arriving at reasonably accurate estimates on the basis of the observations of the Spanish. The observations of Colón on the first voyage are especially suspect (Henige 1978a) because Colón did not venture far inland from the coast and because his group's presence attracted people to the coast to see the ships and the strange foreigners. While Henige's critique of Cook and Borah's (1971) figures suggests that they are too high, he does not suggest another population estimate himself, arguing that "it is futile to offer any numerical estimates at all on the basis of the evidence now before us" (Henige 1978a:237). Based on the textual evidence used by Cook and Borah, and using a similar method of extrapolating backward from the early 1500s, when better population numbers are available, Zambardino (1978:702–4) argues for a 1492 population of around one million people.

While I find Zambardino's estimate reasonable, I feel that this problem is one which will require both the existing ethnohistorical data and regional archaeological survey in the future before we will be able to make real headway (Wilson 1986). The events described in this book certainly indicate the mobility of the Taíno population, either in fleeing the Spanish or in congregating around them, making estimates based on eyewitness accounts even more problematic. With Sauer (1966) and Henige (1978a), I am sufficiently skeptical of the quality of the ethnohistorical observations of population numbers to attempt to estimate the size of Hispaniola's population in 1492.

Those arguing the case of the Indians, especially Las Casas, have blamed the tribute system for the population disaster of the last five years of the fifteenth century. Las Casas describes the terms of the Colón's demands as follows:

The Admiral imposed on all of the *vecinos* of the province of Cibao and all those of the Vega Real and all near the mining areas, everyone fourteen years old and older, that every three months they were to produce a *cascabel* of Flandes, that is to say, a hawksbell [about 85 g, or 3 oz], full of gold dust (only the king Manicaotex[2] had to give a calabash half-full of gold, weighing three *marcos*, which was worth 150 *pesos de oro* or *castellanos*); everyone else who was not from around the mining areas was required to give an *arroba* [twenty-five pounds] of cotton each. (*Historia*, I:417)

He argues passionately that it would have been too great a punishment even for the Turks or Moors or Huns or Vandals, who had oppressed and killed Christians, and more ludicrous still for the fragile Taíno.

The tribute system imposed by Colón certainly contributed to the demographic decline on the island. Collecting gold took labor away from cultivation, hunting, and fishing; although the pre-Hispanic economy of the Greater Antilles does not seem to have required a great deal of labor in any particular season, it did require constant day-to-day labor for cultivation, harvesting, processing the manioc to remove toxins, and replanting (Cassá 1984; DeBoer 1975; Roosevelt 1980; Sturtevant 1961). Moreover, the tribute system may have forced people to plant cotton in plots that had been cleared for *conucos* containing manioc and the other plants, lowering the amount of manioc/cassava or other foods produced.

There were less obvious effects of the tribute system. The imposition of tribute on fear of death evoked a greater sense of terror onto the Taíno society during this period. Because they could not feed themselves in centralized Spanish settlements, large numbers of conquistadores spread out into the villages of Hispaniola. Each was intent on establishing a personal fortune in gold, preferably in secret to avoid paying the "royal fifth" (Wilson 1985a).[3] The most likely way of doing so was by extorting additional gold from the Indians in their vicinity. The cacique Guarionex repeatedly

---

[2]The Adelantado received tribute from Manicavex, one of the "neighbors" of Guarionex, in June of 1496. "The Adelantado remained there the whole month of June, and obtained from the caciques, not only the sum total of the tribute, but also provisions necessary to support himself and the 400 men of his escort" (Martyr 1970:116).

[3]This exacerbated the friction between the Colón family and other Spanish factions, since keeping gold from the crown also required keeping it from the Colón family.

offered to plant *conucos* from the north coast of Hispaniola to the south. Since the Indians were feeding everyone anyway, shifting his tribute obligation from gold to food could only improve his people's situation.

The greatest cause of the population disaster on Hispaniola, however, was the combined effect of disease and starvation. In contrast to the Caribbean's relative isolation from disease, post-medieval Europe was a clearing house for what LeRoy Ladurie has called a "'common market' of microbes" which "passed through a particularly intense, rapid, dramatic, one might even say apocalyptic phase, during the period roughly 1300–1600" (1981:30). Although Europe had experienced a series of major epidemics (most notably one brought on by an East African bacillus in the sixth century A.D.), the greatest European plagues followed the unification of a large part of Asia and parts of Europe by the Mongols, from A.D. 1200 to 1260. Between A.D. 1345 and 1355 the European population was cut nearly in half by the combination of pneumonic and bubonic plagues (p. 44). By the same trans-Asian trade routes, as well as the more familiar routes into Africa, Europe possessed in some measure nearly every Old World disease. The Caribbean, of course, had its own complement of parasites and diseases, and the mortality rate for the conquistadores was high.

The effects of introducing these Old World diseases were catastrophic for the entire New World, but the impact was especially concentrated on Hispaniola. Other than missions of exploration, the colonization of the New World had a relatively slow start. Even the occupation of Puerto Rico, Cuba, and Jamaica did not take place until the early 1500s, after the population of Hispaniola had been drastically reduced. Santo Domingo remained the principal New World port into the 1520s, when the conquest of Mexico began.

Closely interrelated with the impact of these diseases was a famine which occurred during most of 1495 and 1496. Its cause is not obvious. There was a hurricane in October 1495, but in the accounts of the chroniclers, there is no clear correlation between it and the food shortage. Instead, most of the observers reported the famine in a fantastic and paranoid manner as an Indian plot to get rid of the Spanish. Martyr's comments are representative of the evaluation of the famine.

[The Admiral] was informed that the natives suffered from such a severe famine that more than 50,000 men had already perished, and that people continued to die daily as do cattle in time of pest.

This calamity was the consequence of their own folly; for when they saw that the Spaniards wished to settle in their island, they thought they might expel them by creating a scarcity of food. They, therefore, decided not only to plant no more crops, but also to destroy and tear up all the various kinds of cereals used for bread which had already been sown. . . . This was to be done by the people in each district, and especially in the mountainous region of Cipangu and Cibao; that was the country where gold was found in abundance, and the natives were aware that the principal attraction which kept the Spaniards in Hispaniola was gold. At that time the Admiral sent an officer with a troop of armed men to reconnoiter the southern coast of the island, and this officer reported that the regions he had visited had suffered to such an extent from the famine, that during six days he and his men had eaten nothing but the roots of herbs and small plants, or such fruits as grow on the trees. Guarionex, whose territory had suffered less than the others, distributed some provisions amongst our people. (Martyr 1970:108).

In the European consciousness, even through the period of the great European epidemics, there was no real understanding of disease or of the diffusion of microbes and viruses through contact. Humidity and an unusual diet were their principal suspects in the deaths of both Indians and Spaniards. Even Las Casas discounted the importance of disease and appears to have believed the story that the Indians stopped agriculture production.

Many villages decided to try to improve their situation by means of a scheme or trick . . . which was this . . . : they would not plant or make their *conucos*, so that no fruits would grow at all in the land, and they would hide in the mountains where there are many roots, which are called *guayaros*, very nice to eat, and which grow there wild, and there they would also catch the *hutías*, or rabbits, the mountains and valleys are full of, and there get along as well as they could in their unfortunate circumstances. They gained little by this trick, because even though the Christians suffered from terrible hunger and hunted down and persecuted the sad Indians and underwent the greatest trials and danger, they neither left nor died (although as I mentioned, some did die) before all of the misery and calamity came back to rest on the same Indians, because as it happened they were so relentlessly persecuted and pursued with their wives and children up into the hills—so tired, hungry, and harassed that they had no place left to hunt or fish or gather their own kinds of food, and because of the humidity of the mountains and the rivers, where they always went when they fled the Christians, there went with them disease, death, and misery, and an infinite number of fathers and mothers and children died in anguish. Just as if they had been killed in the wars, they died of hunger and sickness that surrounded them, and the fatigue and oppression that followed, and the misery and great pain which encompassed the whole situation. After the period from 1494 to 1496, it is my belief, no more than a third remained of the multitudes that had been on the island. (*Historia*, I:419–20)

What are we to make of this? It seems unlikely that the legend was true in all of its particulars. Martyr mentions that the famine and disease also occurred in the southern part of the island, where very few Spaniards were living. There would have been little inducement for those people to starve themselves to death. Moreover, if it were an islandwide plot, it would presuppose a far greater degree of political organization and coercive power than can be attributed to the Taíno on present evidence. It seems more likely that the famine legend recorded in the chronicles reflects the Europeans' colonial paranoia and their misunderstanding of epidemic diseases. Unfortunately, their lack of understanding of diseases or concern with symptoms gives us very little concrete detail with which to reconstruct exactly what diseases killed the Taíno (although smallpox and measles are strong possibilities; Dobyns 1983:257–58; Ramenofsky 1987).

One intriguing possibility (difficult to substantiate) is that the famine and epidemic of 1495 and 1496 were in part the result of a failure in the food production system (Sauer 1966). Cassava is grown all year round; new plants are started as the mature tubers are harvested, with up to a year's growing time in between. A failure to replant cassava will have its impact up to a year later. It is a possibility (and not much more) that the settlement of Isabela and the first entradas to the interior in 1494, the founding of the first inland forts, and the first battles toward the end of that year, had such a disruptive effect that there was a lapse in the cassava production cycle. This may have had its main impact in 1495, when the epidemic and famine were most severe.

Attempting to come to grips with the tremendous loss of life, some of the chroniclers claimed a high suicide rate among the Indians. Benzioni's account mirrors Las Casas's and others.

Wherefore many went to the woods and there hung themselves, after
having killed their children, saying it was far better to die than to
live so miserably, serving such and so many ferocious tyrants and
wicked thieves. The women, with the juice of a certain herb, dissi-
pated their pregnancy, in order not to produce children, and then
following the example of their husbands, hung themselves. Some
threw themselves from high cliffs down precipices; others jumped
into the sea; others again into rivers; and others starved themselves
to death. Sometimes they killed themselves with their flint knives;
others pierced their bosoms or their sides with pointed stakes. Finally, out of the two millions of original inhabitants, through the
number of suicides and other deaths, occasioned by the oppressive
labour and cruelties imposed by the Spaniards, there are not a hundred and fifty now to be found. (Benzioni 1857:77–78)

Suicide undoubtedly existed, but there is no way to measure
its overall effect on the collapse of the population. Battles yet to
come—in 1497 and 1498—give evidence that the Taíno had by
no means given up entirely. The consideration of suicide by the
various authors is another case of trying to understand a catastrophic phenomenon in familiar terms. In this, there was also
a subtle shifting of blame to the Indians; suicide and abortion
were mortal sins in fifteenth century Christian dogma.

Ferdinand Colón's view of the forces impelling history called
for no such subtlety.

The admiral attributed the ease with which he had discomfited so
vast a multitude, with only 200 ill armed and half-sick men, to the
interposition of Providence. . . . It pleased the Divine Majesty, not
only to enable him to reduce the whole country under authority, but
to send such a scarcity of provisions, and such violent diseases
among the natives, that they were reduced to a third of the number
which they had been when first discovered: Thus making it evident
that such miraculous victories, and the subduing of nations, are the
gift of Providence, and not the effect of our power or good conduct,
or of the want of courage of the natives. (Columbus 1824:130)

The Night of the Fourteen Caciques

By the spring of 1497 Concepción de La Vega was at the center of two conflicts. The first was between two factions of

Spaniards–one led by Bartolomé, the Adelantado; the other led by Francisco de Roldán, the next-highest ranking Spaniard on the island. The other conflict was between the many cacicazgos of the Vega Real and the tribute system as embodied in the Spanish forces. In May of 1497 Roldán and his itinerant group had marched from Isabela to Concepción de La Vega with the intention of taking the blockhouse and controlling the center of the island. Roldán decided that the attack could not succeed and stayed with his company at the nearby village of a cacique called Marque. Within a few weeks a coalition of fourteen caciques assembled to make war on the Spaniards in the Vega Real. Word of this and of Roldán's movements brought the Adelantado and all of the troops he could gather—over 300—into the Vega. In a breach of Taíno battle etiquette that was completely effective for its novelty, the Adelantado led a nighttime raid against several surrounding villages and captured the fourteen most important Indian leaders, including Guarionex.

The records of these events, although lacking in detail, offer additional insight into the sociopolitical organization of the Taíno of the Vega Real. Specifically, the revolt of the fourteen caciques shows the importance of confederacies and collective action among the caciques. This contradicts the chroniclers' model, and that of most later scholars, of monarchical Taíno kingdoms led by single men (e.g. Cassá 1974, 1984; Charlevoix 1731–33; Roth 1887). These events also give some measure of the limitations that existed on a cacique's power. Finally, they contribute a little information to our understanding of the political geography of the Vega Real.

The cacique Guarionex was a pivotal character in the conquest period in the Vega Real, from the destruction of Navidad to his capture in the summer of 1498. As long as he was able, he manipulated the Spaniards expertly. Colón installed a Jeronomite friar named Ramón Pané in Guarionex's village, and from Pané's brief account of the religion of the Taíno, there is an impression of Guarionex and his family.

> The Lord Admiral told me that the language of the province Magdalena Maroris [where Pané was living] was different from the other and that the speech there was not understood throughout the land and that therefore I should go and reside with another principal cacique named Guarionex, lord of a numerous people whose language was understood everywhere in the land.
>
> We then went with that cacique Guarionex almost two years giv-

ing him instruction all the time in our holy faith and the customs of Christians. In the beginning he showed us a good will and gave us hopes that he would do everything we wished and of desiring to be a Christian asking us to teach him the Lord's Prayer, the *Ave Maria* and the Creed. . . . But later he became offended and gave up that good plan through the fault of some other principal men of that country, who blamed him because he was willing to give heed to the Christian law, since the Christians were bad men and got possession of their lands by force. Therefore they advised him to care no more for anything belonging to the Christians, and that they should agree and conspire to slay them, because they could not satisfy them and were resolved not to try in any fashion to follow their ways. (Quoted in Bourne 1906:28–29)

Upon being rejected by Guarionex, Pané left, and the shrine and Christian images he left there were destroyed. The men responsible were caught and burned alive, but "all this did not deter Guarionex and his subjects from the evil design they had of slaying the Christians on the day appointed for bringing in the tribute which they paid" (p. 30). Pané unfortunately gives no further detail about Guarionex and his household, except to add that Guarionex's mother "was the worst woman I knew in those parts" (p. 30).

Martyr also presents the view that Guarionex was partially coerced in his decision to participate in the abortive rebellion.

[The Adelantado] learned . . . that Guarionex had been chosen by the other caciques as their commander-in-chief. Although he had already tested and had reason to fear our arms and tactics, he allowed himself to be partly won over. The caciques had planned a rising of about 15,000 men, armed in their fashion, for a fixed day, thus making a new appeal to the fortunes of battle. (Martyr 1970:122)

Las Casas draws the same conclusion, but adds that it may have been a single rival who affected Guarionex's position.

Guarionex, since he was a man who was naturally good and peaceful and also prudent, and had seen or knew of the power of the Christians and the speed of their horses, and of what had been done to the king Caonabo and to his provinces and to many others of the provinces in the Cibao, had refused to join the rebellion many times, but in the end, harassed and perhaps threatened by another capitán, came with great difficulty to accept it. (*Historia*, I:445)

The raid in which the leaders of the rebellion were captured further demonstrates the Adelantado's ability to understand and exploit Taíno practices. Apparently several villages near Concepción were attacked simultaneously by groups of Spaniards. "Captains were thus sent against the caciques, and surprising them in their sleep, before their scattered subjects could collect, invaded their houses which were unprotected either by ditches, walls, or entrenchments; they attacked and seized them, binding them with cords and bringing them, as they had been ordered, to the Adelantado (Martyr 1970:122).

The account given by Las Casas is more detailed and carries the narrative into the next day, when many of the assembled Indians came to ask for the release of their leaders.

> Don Bartolomé arrived with his people at the fortaleza of Bonao, and from there left, traveling overnight to the fortaleza of Concepción, a good ten leagues distant. Going out with all the people, healthy and sick, to strike the fifteen thousand Indians who were with the king Guarionex and many other allied leaders, and since these sad people lived peacefully, without quarrels and fighting, they did not need walls or fortifications [barbacanas] or moats around their villages. The Christians fell upon them suddenly, at midnight, for the Indians do nothing by night, neither attack nor even prepare for war—they did not even have the time to get their weapons. All in all, they could do nothing against the Spaniards, who did them great damage. The Christians captured the king Guarionex and many others; they killed many of the captured leaders, from those who appeared to have been the instigators, not with any other punishment (I have no doubt) except by burning them alive, for this is what was commonly done. . . . They took the prisoners to the fortaleza Concepción, and five thousand men arrived, all without weapons, wailing and very upset, crying bitter tears, begging that they be given their king Guarionex and their other leaders, fearing that they would be killed or burned alive. Don Bartolomé, having compassion for them and seeing their piety for their natural leaders, and knowing the innate goodness of Guarionex, who was more inclined to put up with and suffer with tolerance the aggravations and injuries done by the Christians, rather than think of or take vengeance, Bartolomé gave them their king and other leaders. (*Historia*, I:445–46)

Martyr reports that the Adelantado captured Guarionex personally and brought him and thirteen others to Concepción. Two of them, the ones who had "corrupted Guarionex and the others, and who had favoured the revolt" (Martyr p. 122) were killed.

As recorded by Las Casas, a portion of the collected army came the next day to ask the release of the captives, which was granted. Martyr gives a more cogent reason for the Adelantado's decision.

> Guarionex and the rest were released, for the Adelantado feared that the natives, affected by the death of the caciques, might abandon their fields, which would have occasioned a grievous damage to our people, because of the crops. About six thousand of their subjects had come to solicit their freedom. . . . The Adelantado spoke to Guarionex and the other caciques, and by means of promises, presents and threats, charged them to take good care for the future to engage in no further revolt. Guarionex made a speech to the people, in which he praised our power, our clemency to the guilty, and our generosity to those who remained faithful; he exhorted them to calm their spirits and for the future neither to think nor to plan any hostilities against the Christians, but rather to be obedient, humble and serviceable to them, unless they wished worse things to overtake them. When he had finished his speech, his people took him on their shoulders in a hammock and in this wise they carried him to the village where he lived, and within a few days the entire country was pacified. (P. 122)

It was more than a consideration of the disruption of tribute that made the Adelantado grant clemency to the caciques. There were still many thousand desperate Indians surrounding them, and in the two years since the first battle of the Vega Real, they had gained experience of the Spaniard's vulnerabilities. Bartolomé's midnight raid was conceived in the knowledge that the next day's battle might be disastrous. The rebel Roldán, who had already been turned from his intention of taking Concepción, was also waiting in the wings and could have entered the battle on the side of Guarionex, or at least taken the opportunity to contest further the Adelantado's authority.

The most unfortunate gap in the records of these events concerns the identity of the other thirteen caciques and of the relationships between them and Guarionex. The cacique called Marque, with whom Roldán and his men had stayed, is not mentioned by name but may have been involved. His name never reappears in the documents, and it is conceivable that he (encouraged by Roldán) had been one of the instigators who was executed.

Guarionex's superior political and social status relative to the other caciques seems to be genuine, and not just the bias of the reporters. Yet his relationship with the others seems to allow for him to be forced into actions against his will. It is extremely difficult to know the extent to which the rebellion was Guarionex's project. Because of his importance in delivering the tribute of food and gold to the Spaniards, they were unlikely to kill or depose him, so even in the worst case (the one that occurred), he would not lose very much. Had he resisted the others involved in planning the rebellion, however, he might have lost his political base of power.

Guarionex, then, seems to have a status somewhat greater than that of the first among equals, but less than the absolute monarch which the Spaniards perceived him to be. Like Behecchio in the cacicazgo of Xaraguá, he had the authority to negotiate tribute arrangements without consulting anyone but was apparently unable to initiate or veto military action in his own right. His power most likely derived from his ability to convince other leaders through persuasive rhetoric, through appeal to kinship relationships which seem to exist among most of the Taíno elite (Guarionex had offered a sister in marriage to Diego Colón, the Admiral's interpreter), through gifts or displays of generosity in competitive feasts, or through more Machiavellian political maneuvering.

The Flight of Guarionex and the Battle of El Cabrón

The raid on the fourteen caciques subdued the Vega Real for a little more than a year, until the summer of 1498. In this period Guarionex was under attack from three directions. For his inability to defend the people from the Spanish, he was considered ineffective by the other Taíno rulers. He was still required to deliver the same quarterly tribute of food and gold to the Adelantado; in addition the anti-Colón forces of Roldán were staying in the villages of the Vega and probably demanding an equal amount of food and gold for themselves (Wilson 1985a).

As discussed in chapter 4, the Adelantado went to Xaraguá to collect the tribute demanded from Anacaona and Behecchio. He was to return and collect quarterly tribute from Guarionex. Under attack from all sides, Guarionex and a group of family and retainers fled north into the mountains of the Cordillera Septentrional (figure 6). According to Martyr, Guarionex

> took refuge in the mountains which border the northern coast only
> ten leagues to the west of Isabela. Both the mountains and their in-

habitants bear the same name, *Ciguaia* [Las Casas: Ciguayo]. The chief of all the caciques inhabiting the mountain regions is called Maiobanexios [Las Casas: Mayobanex], who lived at a place called Capronus [Las Casas: El Cabrón]. . . . The natives are ferocious and warlike, and it is thought they are of the same race as the cannibals, for when they descend from their mountains to fight with their neighbours in the plain, they eat all whom they kill. It was with the cacique of these mountains that Guarionex took refuge, bringing him gifts, consisting of things which the mountaineers lack. (Martyr 1970:127)

Figure 7. Northeastern Hispaniola, showing the reconstructed linguistic boundaries at the time of contact

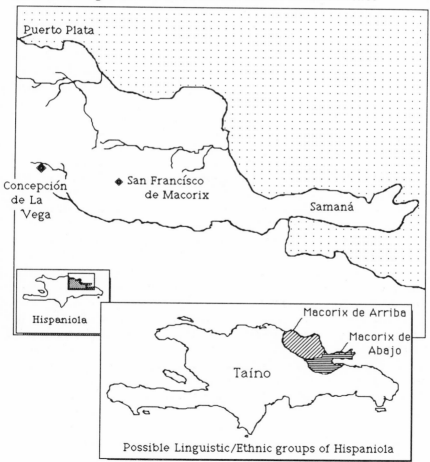

The friar Ramón Pané has already commented about the ethnic and linguistic diversity on the island during the contact period. Pané's first assignment had been in the region around modern San Francisco de Macorix (figure 7), which bears the indigenous name of the region and its people. The people there spoke the language called Macorix, which seems to have been mutually unintelligible with Taíno, although there seems to have been considerable bilingualism. Similarly, *Ciguayo* apparently refers to an ethnic group different from the majority of people on the island. The relationship between Ciguayo and Macorix is unclear; the names may apply to the same group. Finally, from the first voyage the Spaniards noted the difference in language, hair and body decoration, and aggressiveness of the Indians inhabiting the Samaná peninsula in northeast Hispaniola (these were the people Colón's group skirmished with at Bahía de Las Flechas at the end of the first voyage). Las Casas, the most linguistically sensitive of the chroniclers, offers this conclusion:

> There were three distinct languages in this island, which were mutually unintelligible: the first was of the people we called the Lower Macorix, and the other of the people of Upper Macorix, which I described in chapters 2 and 3 as the fourth and sixth provinces. The other language was the universal one for all of the land, and was the most elegant and contained the most words, and was the most sweet in sound. (Las Casas, *Apologética*, II:311)

Figure 7 is reconstructed from the consideration of linguistic boundaries given in the chapters Las Casas mentions.

At present the archaeological data from Hispaniola are not sufficiently developed to try to impose patterns of material culture onto the tentative linguistic map. The first difficulty is determining what sites were occupied at the time of Spanish contact, a task which requires either the excavation of European objects in stratigraphic context or the use of chronological tools more precise than radiocarbon dating. The latter do not yet exist on Hispaniola.

At the level of precision provided by radiocarbon dating, there is evidence that from the beginning of Hispaniola's colonization by ceramic-using people, there were up to three ceramic styles being produced on the island at the same time (cf. Rouse 1986; Veloz Maggiolo 1972). Most of the dated sites are along the southeastern coasts of the Dominican Republic, and even there there is considerable overlap, both spatially and temporally. Unfortunately, there are no similar data from the Vega Real, either in sites excavated or located in archaeological survey.

The Vega Real, is a fault-block valley whose northern edge is an extremely straight and consistent line of weathered hills running from the northwest to the southeast. The escarpment is visible from anywhere in the valley. There is ethnohistorical evidence that the range of hills represented a boundary between the Taíno of the Vega and the Macorix of the hills (Macorix de Arriba, in Las Casas's scheme). Las Casas says that "*Macorix* means something like the word "foreigner" [extraño] or "barbarian" [bárbaro], because [Macorix de Arriba and Macorix de Abajo] were different from each other and different from the normal speech of the island (Las Casas, *Apologética*, I:21). As noted above, Martyr considered them to be of the same race as cannibals, who came down from the hills and ate their captives.

Nevertheless, when Guarionex could no longer survive in the Vega Real, he fled north, bearing gifts, into the country of the cacique Mayobanex. It was enigmatic to the Spaniards that Mayobanex gave Guarionex asylum; they never found adequate justification, although it is extensively discussed, particularly by Las Casas.

> Having missed Guarionex and having seen that many people were missing from the villages and that every day more left, they sent word from Concepción to Santo Domingo to the Adelantado that the king Guarionex was possibly revolting. Receiving the letters, the Adelantado came quickly, since Guarionex was such an important leader and all of his people were mine workers and the majority of the tribute came through him. Taking the ninety healthiest men, the Adelantado went to Concepción. He began there asking the Indians he ran into and others he found where Guarionex had gone; they responded that they did not know; forcing them with threats, and I have no doubts with torture, he discoverd that he was in the land of the Ciguayos with king Mayobanex. (Las Casas, *Historia*, I:458)

Martyr takes a slightly different view of the flight of Guarionex. He says that Guarionex found allies among the Ciguayo and began raiding the Vega, killing whatever Christians they found (Martyr 1970:128). When the Adelantado marched against Mayobanex and the Ciguayo, Martyr says, "It may be truthfully added that about three thousand of the islanders who had suffered from the invasions of the Ciguana tribe, who were their sworn enemies, joined forces with the Spaniards" (p. 143). Some number of Taíno probably accompanied the Adelantado, but in the difficult three-month campaign they are not mentioned again in Las Casas's account.

The initial confrontation with the Ciguayo was a more rigorous fight than the Spaniards were acccustomed to. Martyr gives this vivid description:

> Their appearance is fearsome and repulsive, and they march into
> battle daubed with paint, as did the Thracians and Agathyrses. These
> natives indeed paint themselves from the forehead to the knees, with
> black and scarlet colours which they extract from certain fruits simi-
> lar to pears, and which they carefully cultivate in their gardens.
> Their hair is tormented into a thousand strange forms, for it is long
> and black, and what nature refuses they supply by art. They look
> like goblins emerged from the infernal caverns. (P. 143)

After an uneasy night and another more fierce day of battle, the Adelantado demanded that Guarionex be turned over to him. The Spaniards' persistence seems to have surprised and puzzled the Indians. Guarionex had abdicated his impossible position of placating both the Spaniards and the other Taíno caciques; he had left what persuasive or coercive power he had behind him in the Vega Real. That he was relentlessly pursued over the next three months was apparently senseless, according to native reckoning, and unexpected.

Las Casas presents an account of the deliberations that went on among the Ciguayo that must be utter fiction. As far as is known, the Spaniards had no spies in their camp, as they would have had in the Vega Real, and the speech of Mayobanex is just as Las Casas would have constructed it.

> From among the prisoners the Adelantado sent one to Mayobanex
> to tell him that they did not come to make war on him and his
> people . . . but were only looking for Guarionex, whom it was
> known that Mayobanex had hidden, and if they gave up Guarionex
> they would have friendly relations and they would not be utterly de-
> stroyed. Mayobanex responded, "The Christians have said that Gua-
> rionex is a good man and virtuous; he has never done wrong to any-
> one, as is publicly known; and for this dignity it is compassionate
> to help him in his need, to succor him and defend him. The Chris-
> tians, however, are bad men, tyrants, who want only to usurp the
> land of others and only know how to spill the blood of those who
> have never given offense, and because of this, I have decided that I

do not want your friendship, nor do I want to see you or hear you, and when I had the chance, along with my people, of choosing either the Christians or Guarionex, I took the task of destroying the former and throwing them from the land." (*Historia*, I:459)

Receiving this news, the Adelantado and his ninety men continued to reduce the countryside, burning all of the villages and conucos that they found. Las Casas offers a second, more believable (or at least more culturally sensitive) version of Mayobanex's defense of Guarionex.

Mayobanex put it to his people, who with one voice said to hand over Guarionex. Mayobanex answered that it was illogical to hand over to your enemies one who was a good man and who had never done you any harm, who had always been a friend, and whom they owed a debt because Guarionex had taught Mayobanex and his queen an *areyto* of Magua, that is, to sing the songs of the Vega, where the kingdom of Guarionex is located. And Guarionex had come to him and Mayobanex had promised to guard and defend him and he would not go back on the promise. Mayobanex called up Guarionex and both started to cry. Mayobanex urged them all to be brave and not to fear the Christians. (Pp. 459–60)

The gift, or exchange, of an *areyto* is unusual in the ethnohistoric record from Hispaniola and must have been quite powerful. There is no documentary suggestion of any kinship relationship between the two men, and the gift of an *areyto* may have been a generous and appropriate gift between peers (Helms 1979, 1988).

The guerrilla war went on in the mountains for three months, and the Ciguayo split into small bands and hid in the mountains. Both Indians and Spanish were near starvation, and the Adelantado's men were threatening rebellion because of his obsession with Guarionex. From occasional captives, the Adelantado learned the location of Mayobanex's camp and employed this ruse:

Twelve Christians, completely naked, dyed themselves Indian color—black with red, from a fruit called *bixa*. Taking their guides with great caution, they arrived where Mayobanex was hiding with only his wife and sons and little family. They drew swords which they had hidden in bunches of palms they called *yagmas*, which they carried like people carrying burdens, as the Indians did, and they caught them . . . and took them back to Concepción in chains. (Las Casas, *Historia*, I:460)

Eventually Guarionex was captured as well and jailed in the blockhouse at Concepción de La Vega. Mayobanex died in prison a few years later, and Guarionex lived in chains at Concepción until 1502, when he was sent to Spain. His ship sank in a storm, and he died with all the ship's crew.

Thus ended the affair of Guarionex's flight from the Vega Real, his protection by Mayobanex, the Adelantado's three-month campaign against the Ciguayo, and ultimately the capture of both caciques. The episode started with the Spaniards' misperception of the sociopolitical organization of the Taíno. They believed that Guarionex was a sovereign king, whose power was retained until his death. A more accurate picture seems to be that he was the highest-ranking cacique among several near-equals, who was able to hold together a confederacy for a while. The Adelantado feared a new alliance with the people of the northern mountains, who already raided the plains, and overreacted to the retirement of a leader whose authority was already gone. His obsession with capturing Guarionex provided an excuse to make war against the Ciguayo and reduce that dangerous part of the island.

Summary

Between 1494 and 1498 the sociopolitical structure of the Taíno disintegrated, and this process is illustrated in the events in the Vega Real. The cacique Guarionex was perhaps extraordinary in his ability to manage two competing groups of Spaniards as well as the other indigenous political leaders in the valley. The overwhelming pressures of the situation, however, brought about the collapse of his cacicazgo as well as all of the other indigenous political systems on the island.

The discussion of these events allows a somewhat less murky, although still unclear, view of the political geography of the Vega Real. I have found it impossible to treat these many cacicazgos, or chiefdoms, in the way traditionally used by historians of the Taíno. Las Casas, in several passages, gave verbal descriptions of the political boundaries of the various cacicazgos of the island. The pilot Andrés Morales was ordered by the governor Nicholas de Ovando to prepare a general survey of the island in 1508, and his map is the basis for several reconstructions, including Sauer's (1966). Charlevoix (1731–33), using Las Casas's writing and relying on much second-hand information recorded by Oviedo y Valdez (1959), produced another scheme of cacicazgo bound-aries, which has survived as the standard interpretation. Bernardo Vega (1980) has another partition of the island in the context of a reanalysis of these written sources and early maps. His recon-struction, together with Charlevoix's (1731–33) and Rouse's (1948), is depicted in figure 8.

The characterization of the Taíno chiefdoms that emerges from the ethnohistorical sources, notwithstanding the conceptualiza-tions of Las Casas, Morales, Oviedo, and other witnesses, is not one of political entities that can be neatly bounded on a map. The conquistadores saw the Taíno through the eyes of early mod-ern Europeans. They interpreted tales of places like Caonabo's province *Maguana* or Guarionex's *Magua* in terms of European feudal kingdoms whose boundaries (at any point in time) were known. For the Taíno, if there were such rigid categories, they were not recovered in the historical documents.

In the case of Guarionex, the area over which he may have exercised some economic control (which contributed to his feasts or paid him with some fraction of their production) might have been one thing; the area under his military leadership (from which he might draw warriors) might be quite another. Particularly in the latter case, the boundary is drawn largely on the basis of imme-diate circumstances. The fifteen thousand warriors (or whatever part thereof in the actual event) that assembled around Concep-ción before the night of the Adelantado's raid on the fourteen caciques were not all his subjects but rather were partners (or subjects of his partners) in a cooperative venture. In the episode of Guarionex's asylum among the people of Mayobanex, we see that this fluidity of boundaries transcends linguistic and ethnic lines as well.

This is not to say, however, that the Taíno chiefdoms have no spatial referents at all. The problem lies in trying to identify some limit at the periphery, not in locating an approximate center or core area. For the most important chieftainships (as reflected in the histories), these can be roughly located on a map (figure 8). The point to be stressed is that the kinds of geographical bound-aries of the Taíno chiefdoms that can be drawn on a map are inappropriate to the transient nature of the political structures.

Figure 8. Reconstructed cacicazgo boundaries

Locations of the Major Taíno Cacicazgos
in 1492

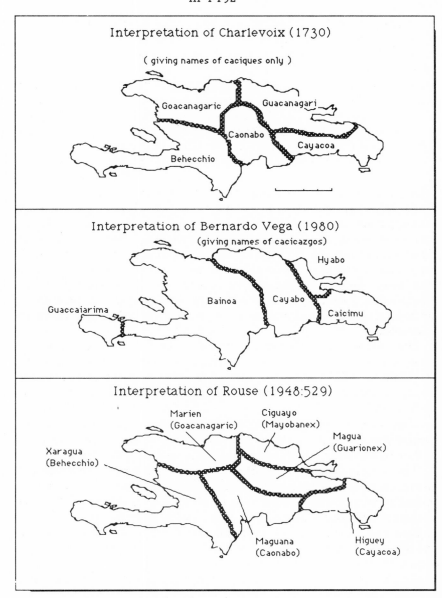

4

✳✳✳✳✳✳

The Adelantado's Visit
to Xaraguá

The ethnohistorical accounts of the visit of Colón's brother Barto-lomé—the Adelantado, or governor, by title—to the province of Xaraguá are remarkable for their sensitive portrayal of a contact situation. More, they offer insights into the operations of historical processes which are critical for understanding Taíno social structure and political organization. At issue are the ways in which the Taíno elite acted within the context of their own political boundaries, how they related with other cacicazgos, and how these social relations may have been significant in producing cultural change.

The events discussed here occurred in late 1496 and early 1497. The Adelantado's initial visit to the province probably occurred in January 1497, and he returned to Xaraguá for a short stay in April of that year. Bartolomé had arrived on Hispaniola in June 1494, and so had been on the island for two years and seven months. Of the people with him, no Europeans had been on the island for more than three years, and most had arrived after— either in October 1494, October 1495, or July 1496.

The events discussed in this chapter depict the sociopolitical structure of the Taíno as dynamic and mutable, subject to transformation through the competition of elites and of polities. The ethnohistorical data suggest that elite interaction (in many forms) across the boundaries of political units was a significant factor in the restructuring and reorganization of the Caribbean chiefdoms from generation to generation.

At the level of ethnohistorical detail provided in the accounts of the Adelantado's trip, we can see several very suggestive patterns. It appears that the structure of a cacique's polygynous marriages was a powerful tool in concentrating social and political status in his lineage. It also seems probable that when no acceptable mates were available for the highest-ranking women within their own polity, that marriage to a high-ranking man in a neighboring cacicazgo was possible. Coupled with documentary evidence for Taíno succession and inheritance patterns, it is suggested that the structure and principles of the Taíno sociopolitical organization were conducive to the consolidation of political units. In fact, the Spaniards may have been witnesses to such an event. The engimatic details concerning the woman Anacaona are central to all of these questions.

The Spanish Dilemma

Through the first decade of the occupation of Hispaniola, the Spaniards were continually faced with the problem of provisioning more than a few men in any one place for more than a very short period. Colón's dream of establishing port cities had failed twice by the summer of 1496, first with the catastrophe of Navidad, which was completely destroyed upon his return on the second voyage, and then with the town of Isabela, also on the north coast. Large settlements were found to be traps of disease and starvation. The Spaniards, primarily minor nobility and soldiers, were unable to feed themselves with their attempted transplant of a European economy, and Colón's plan of temporarily provisioning the colonies with a supply line from Spain was doomed.

The Taíno economy was based on a range of wild and cultivated starches which were harvested as they were needed, and on fish, eels, iguanas, and the small rodent hutia, none of which were stored for long periods (Sturtevant 1961).[1] With very little stored food to commandeer, there remained the option of increasing production on the local level manyfold in order to feed the foreigners. Even in the cases where the local Indians were inclined or compelled to attempt it, however, the production of manioc could not quickly be increased; while both planting and harvesting went

---

[1]Some foods were preserved and stored for at least short periods. Martyr reports an encounter with fishermen who were "sent to fish by their cacique, who was preparing a festival for the reception of another chief. . . . When asked why they cooked the fish they were to carry to their cacique, they replied that they did so to preserve it from corruption" (Martyr 1970:95).

on in all seasons, each plant could take more than a year to mature. Other food sources, such as wild foods, garden horticultural products, and possibly maize could be produced more quickly, but each avenue for increasing the food supply involved increasing the amount of effort put into food production on the short run (Roosevelt 1980). In practice, it appears that the Spaniards could weather this production lag only by staying in small, widely dispersed groups (Wilson 1985b). To maintain a large company of men, they had to travel constantly.

Between 1494 and 1497 Colón compromised between the need to distribute his men and the need for protection from the increasingly hostile Taíno by building a chain of small forts from Isabela into the interior (figure 9). When Colón went to Spain in March 1496 to attempt to stem the erosion of his royal and commercial support, his brother Bartolomé, the Adelantado by title, continued this process by establishing a blockhouse in the vicinity of the mines at San Christobal.

In July of that year three caravels arrived at Isabela, bearing a disappointing cargo of partially rotten salt pork, grain, oil, and wine. They also carried Colón's instructions to establish a southern port town nearer to the new goldfields, at the mouth of the Ozama River, the site of modern Santo Domingo. Leaving only ten men at Isabela, those too sick to travel and shipwrights building two new caravels, the Adelantado and his company of over a hundred men went to the south coast.

The territory around Santo Domingo, also densely populated, proved more hospitable than the richer but more militant Vega Real, and in contrast to the undercurrent of Spanish dissent throughout the island at this time, reports from Santo Domingo were usually very positive (Martyr 1970:117; Las Casas, *Historia* I:440). In two months, however, perhaps reaching the point at which such a large company could no longer continue to be supported, the Adelantado took Indian guides and a troop of about a hundred men and marched west to visit the famous kingdom of Xaraguá.

It is unclear whether, or to what extent, these explorers knew of the region of Xaraguá. The name was probably known. In exculpating himself for the destruction of Navidad, the apparently minor cacique Guacanagarí in turn blamed several of the important caciques of the island, most notably Caonabo, cacique of the region the Adelantado's company was crossing. For this and other real and imagined crimes, including an attack on the forta-

Figure 9. Spanish forts on Hispaniola before 1500

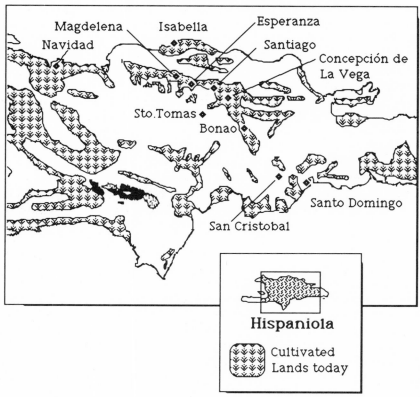

leza at Santo Tomás, Caonabo "a man well up in years, experienced and of a most piercing wit and much knowledge," according to the Admiral [Columbus 1824:132–33]) had been considered by the Spaniards to be the most dangerous of the Indian leaders. He had been captured the year before the Adelantado's march and had died in transit to Spain. The woman Anacaona, sister of the cacique of Xaraguá and wife of Caonabo, was probably also known to Bartolomé, at least in name.

The Boundaries of Xaraguá

Arriving at the Río Neiba (figure 10), 145 km (90 mi) west of Santo Domingo, the company temporarily split. One group went south and discovered stands of mahogany, probably in the Bahía de Neiba, which they cut and stashed in the houses of Indians there. The Adelantado's party was soon met by a large army led by Behecchio Anacaochoa.

Why was Behecchio on the banks of the Neiba, 153 km (95 mi) away from his home? Las Casas says that "it appeared that the king Behecchio had news that the Christians were coming, and having heard the news that the Christians were coming, and having heard the news of their works against the king Caonabo and that which had been done against his kingdom, sent certain

Figure 10. The area of Xaraguá

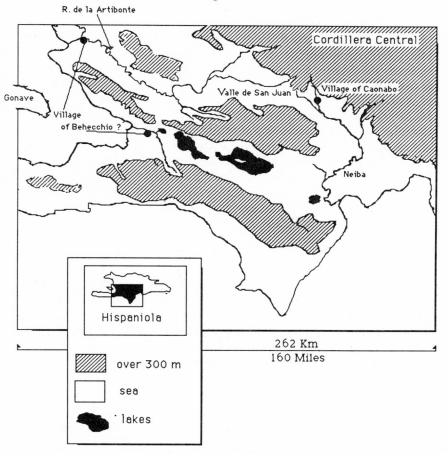

people or came himself in person with his child's play to resist them" (*Historia*, I:441). It is certainly possible that this was Behecchio's intention. The whereabouts of the Adelantado's force was of course a critical concern for all the Taíno caciques, and its movements were always anticipated.

Martyr takes another view. "During this time the Adelantado, who had marched to the right, had encountered at a place not far from the river Neiba a powerful cacique, named Beuchios Anacauchoa, who was at that time engaged in an expedition to conquer the people along the river, as well as some other caciques of the island" (1970:118). Other circumstances also lend credence to Martyr's story. The Río Neiba was far beyond any of the various reconstructions of the pre-Columbian political boundaries of Xaraguá. It is considered, on good evidence, to be in Caonabo's province, the one called Maguana. The mouth of the Neiba was the downstream port from Caonabo's village at the modern Corrales de los Indios (figure 10). The eastern boundary of Xaraguá was probably the watershed between the Valle de San Juan and that of the Rivière de l'Artibonite, the modern boundary between Haiti and the Dominican Republic.

Following the capture of Caonabo the year before, the political situation in the western parts of the island seems to have been rather fluid. Behecchio and the caciques of Xaraguá could have been taking advantage of the generally chaotic state of the island to access this neighboring territory. The implication that this was an accession by military force, however, may not be accurate.

Succession and Inheritance among the Elite

The woman Anacaona, Behecchio's sister, was by royal marriage the wife of the late Caonabo. The details of this relationship (whether she was his highest-ranking wife, whether they had children) are not known, but coupling this intermarriage between the two polities with a general knowledge of Taíno rules of succession and inheritance allows further speculation on the presence of Behecchio and his army on the banks of the Neiba.

The phenomenon of politically and socially motivated elite intermarriage is widely known in the Antilles and elsewhere. It is a common characteristic of a political environment of aggressive, competing political units. The practice was certainly familiar to the conquistadores: the marriage of Ferdinand of Aragon to Isabela of Castille united the two largest medieval kingdoms of what was to become (within the years of their reign) the nation-state of Spain.

The impact of this pattern of elite intermarriage on Taíno socio-political structure is closely tied to the difficult issues of inheritance and succession among the Taíno. It is clear, I believe, that the Taíno were a predominately matrilineal society—a person's assignment to kinship categories was made with reference to female lines of descent (Cassá 1974; Fewkes 1970 [1907]; Keegan and Maclachlan 1989; Rouse 1948; Sued Badillo 1979; Wilson 1986). I qualify this statement with the term "predominately" because the ethnohistorical accounts contain a degree of ambiguity about whether chiefly succession always passed from a man to his sister's son. The brief and often contradictory accounts of Las Casas, Oviedo, Martyr, Benzioni, and others offer at once a general outline of the patterns of succession and the impression that the real traditions of succession and inheritance are more complex than we currently understand. Helms's (1980) analysis of succession in the circum-Caribbean chiefdoms illustrates this confusion. She draws the distinction between categories of statuses that could be inherited by virtue of family lines alone and others which were acquired by an individual's own efforts during his or her lifetime. The inheritance rules pertaining to these two categories apparently differed, but in ways we do not wholly understand. There also seem to be different rules of inheritance associated with statuses passing through matrilines and patrilines (i.e. statuses inherited from one's mother and those inherited from one's father; see Helms 1980).

Possibly reflective of this confusion are the morphologically complex names possessed by caciques (as well, not surprisingly, as by the principal Taíno gods). These names undoubtedly contain element's of the cacique's family "pedigree," but they also probably signify (in prefixes and suffixes, if not in the stems themselves) the inherited and acquired statuses of the individual. About the cacique of Xaraguá, Martyr observes:

> Beuchios Anacauchoa was also called *Tareigua Hobin*, which means "prince resplendent as copper." So likewise *Starei*, which means "shining"; *Huibo*, meaning "haughtiness"; *Duyheiniquem*, meaning a "rich river." Whenever Beuchios Anacauchoa publishes an order, or makes his wishes known by heralds' proclamation, he takes great care to have all these names and forty more recited. If, through care-

lessness or neglect, a single one were omitted, the cacique would feel
himself grievously outraged; and his colleagues share this view.
(Martyr 1970:387).

Although complex, the accounts we have agree generally on
the cultural preferences in the succession of caciques. Oviedo y
Valdés (1857:136) states that the cacique's son inherited his title
(the exact extent of this status Oviedo did not specify), and when
no sons were available, the office fell to the son of the cacique's
sister. The explanation for this, dwelled upon by the morally suspi-
cious chroniclers, was that one could be more certain that the
son of a sister was of one's line than the son of a brother's wife.
Benzioni, the master of secondhand information, says that this
custom is so that "they can depend on their being her sons, not
so as to a man's supposed sons. The reason is, that in those countries there is very little chastity" (1857:82–83). A further and perhaps more salient reason for the practice lies in the importance
of the statuses carried through the matriline.

Martyr offers this version of the succession rules:

> The caciques choose as heir to their properties, the eldest son of
> their sister, if such a one exists; and if the eldest sister has no son,
> the child of the second or third sister is chosen. The reason is, that
> this child is bound to be of their blood. They do not consider the
> children of their wives as legitimate. When there are no children of
> their sisters, they choose amongst those of their brothers, and failing
> these, they fall back upon their own. (1970:87)

Martyr offers a further rule, which, if valid, would constitute
another way in which chiefdoms could become consolidated. "If
they themselves have no children, they will their estates to whom-
soever in the island is considered most powerful, that their subjects
may be protected by him against their hereditary enemies" (p.
387).

If the preferred (and predetermined) successor to the cacique
was the son of his sister or, in the absence of such a person, occa-
sionally his own biological son, we are faced with a quite significant prospect when the dying cacique's sister is wed via elite intermarriage to another cacique. If we understand the rules of
succession correctly, her son could stand heir to *both* cacicazgos.
As the sister's son, he could inherit from his uncle; and he could
conceivably inherit from his father (his mother's husband) as well.
The result of this process, and the pattern suggested by Martyr

in which a cacicazgo without a predetermined heir would be willed to the custody of another powerful cacique, would be a system in which chiefdoms could coalesce into fewer, larger, and more inclusive polities.

This leaves aside the issue of whether the wife of the dying cacique could succeed him as a ruler, either in her own right or as regent for a young son. Alegría's (1979) compilation of the historical references to caciques from Puerto Rico led him to conclude that the presence of cacicas, or female caciques (to which there are many historical references), was either illusory or the product of the collapsing sociopolitical structure under Spanish occupation. This view has been contradicted by Sued Badillo (1985), who, citing the ethnological importance of matrilines in the residence, inheritance, and succession rules in South American Indian groups, argues that female leadership of political units was common among the Taíno of the Antilles. Far from reaching any resolution, this problem points again to the complex mixture of achieved and inherited statuses (inherited through both matriline and patriline) which were the requisites for a Taíno cacique.

If Behecchio was on a mission of conquest or pacification, it is possible that it was on the behalf of (or legitimized by) his sister Anacaona or her son, if she had one. Also, it is possible that he was taking advantage of the leadership crisis in Maguana following Caonabo's death. If so, it appears to have been a relatively bloodless conquest begun, and facilitated, by an astute marriage alliance. In any case, on the banks of the Neiba, he and the Adelantado managed to avoid battle, and both groups proceeded west through the former territory of Caonabo to Xaraguá.

Elite Hospitality

The treatment of the Adelantado and his company in Xaraguá is the best view available of elite hospitality among the Taíno, of a "state visit," for such it was in both Bartolomé's and Behecchio's eyes. In its structure and scheduling, it probably followed very closely the pattern of a royal visit by another Taíno cacique. From many other instances and references the importance of this kind of hospitality among the Taíno is clear, but in almost every case, circumstances—paranoia and overreaction on one or both parts—prevented the unfolding of events in their traditional pattern. By this time Bartolomé was perhaps more sensitive than the other leaders to the ways of the islanders, far more so than his brother. He was reputed by Martyr and Las Casas to be adept at the Arawakan language, and he had with him Indian translators with several years' experience.

Arriving at Xaraguá, they were met with an elaborate welcome.

> Out came infinite people and many señores and nobility, whose seats were of all the province of the king Behecchio and the queen, his sister, Anacaona, singing their songs and dancing their dances, which they called *areytos*, things that were very pleasant and agreeable to see, especially when their numbers were great. Out came thirty women, who were kept as wives of the king Behecchio, all completely naked, only covering their private parts with half-skirts of cotton, white and very elaborate in their style of weaving, which they call *naguas*, which cover from the belt to the middle of the leg; they were carrying green branches in their hands, singing and dancing and jumping with moderation, as is suitable for women, and showing great peace, delight, happiness, and the spirit of a party. They all arrived in front of Don Bartolomé Colón, and they went down on their knees on the earth, with great reverence, and gave him the branches and palms which they carried in their hands. (Las Casas, *Historia*, I:441)

The fortuitous symbolism of their gesture, whether construed as olive branches of peace or palms at the gates of Jerusalem, was not missed by the Christians. The symbolic meaning of the branches within the Taíno culture is not known, but if it was a statement of peaceful intentions and hospitality, it was so received.

The high-ranking individuals, implied by Las Casas and Martyr to constitute a second tier of authority in the political organization of Xaraguá,[2] were there for a number of reasons. The collective experience of the Taíno had been that the presence of a large group of cavalry and foot soldiers on the march preceded battle of some sort, and so they had come or were summoned with their people as a military force. Also, the region of Xaraguá was the last major chiefdom from which tribute had not been demanded. Behecchio undoubtedly expected that this was the Adelantado's intent and, by the evidence of his welcome, saw appeasement as the best policy.

---

[2]Las Casas: "muchos señores y nobleza, que se ayuntaron de toda la provincia con el rey Behecchio y la reina" (*Historia*, I:441).

What the lesser caciques' voices counted in the negotiations Behecchio was to conduct apparently single-handedly—how political and economic power was distributed in Xaraguá, in other words—is unclear and will be discussed below.

Upon their arrival at Behecchio's village, the Spaniards were remarkably relaxed and unsuspicious. They were feted in a grand style with fish of the rivers and sea and, most remarkably to the commentators, on iguana, always considered repugnant to the Spanish. Perhaps the most telling measure of the relaxation of normal military discipline is that they were taken by twos and threes to sleep in the various houses of the village. It is difficult to assess the unconventionality of this move in the absence of comparable instances, but through Martyr's interviews with participants, the Adelantado certainly had considered the possibility that Behecchio's forces could have killed them all.

Of course the welcome could very well have been even more congenial than is related by Las Casas and Martyr; they dwell uncharacteristically on the beauty of the Xaraguán women.

> As for the young girls, they covered no part of their bodies, but wore their hair loose upon their shoulders and a narrow ribbon tied around the forehead. Their face, breasts, hands, and the entire body was quite naked, and of a somewhat brunette tint. All were beautiful, so that one might think he beheld those splendid naiads or nymphs of the fountains, so much celebrated by the ancients. (Martyr 1970:119–20)

But the welcome received by the Spaniards, at least as it is represented in the chronicles, does not appear to be of the same class as that which the British received in the Sandwich Isles, where "[the Hawaiian women] would almost use violence to force you into their Embrace whether we gave them anything or not" (Beaglehole 1967:1085). To the Taíno, the Spanish were an ambiguous class of being—supernatural perhaps, but actors in the island's political drama as well. The terms of address used for the Spanish captains were usually those reserved for caciques. For caciques they were brothers, and for commoners, lords. In their intercultural sexual negotiations this god/man ambiguity is always evident: what in Hawaii (briefly) was reproduction by gods was in the Caribbean a form of political maneuvering and social climbing.

Archaeologically, we do not know exactly where the village of Behecchio and Anacaona was located or what it looked like. There are, however, only a few places where the village could have been located, given the comments made in the documents and the geography of the area. The island of Hispaniola is at the axis of two branches of the North American cordillera system (Blume 1974:211). The northern branch, including the major Cordillera Central of the Dominican Republic, is an extension of the Sierra de las Minas (also gold bearing) of Guatemala and the Maya Mountains in Belize. It crosses the Caribbean Sea as the Cayman Ridge, above water at the Cayman Islands, and forms Cuba's only real mountain chain, the Sierra Maestra on the southeast corner. The second ridge extends from the Sierra Isabela in Nicaragua across the shallows to the Blue Mountains of Jamaica and produces the Guayacanilla peninsula of southwestern Haiti.

In southern Hispaniola a large block fault separates the two chains, and in it, below sea level, lies the salt lakes Enriquillo and Etang Saumatre. In this system of valleys and ridges that trend northwest to southeast, there are two possibilities for the location of the village of Behecchio. The first and most likely is in the Cul-de-Sac plain of Haiti, now the site of Port-au-Prince; the second possibility is one valley to the north, at the mouth of the Rivière de l'Artibonte, 96 km (60 mi) distant. Both areas are highly developed, and no archaeological evidence for Behecchio's seat yet exists.

From the descriptions of events that took place in the village, however, and by analogy with other places on the island visited by the Spaniards, we can gather something of the physical structures in the village. There was a plaza, probably the same as the bateyes, or ball courts, known archaeologically. This was mentioned as a site of public displays, for singing *aryeto*s and dancing, and as the site of a staged battle—but not, in this visit, as a place where the ball game was played. There was the house of Behecchio, where feasts were held and where Bartolomé and six others were lodged with Behecchio and some of his people. If we take the estimate of one hundred Spaniards in the company and take Las Casas's estimate of two to three soldiers to a house, there may have been thirty or forty other houses in the village. The village was on a river, but six miles from the sea. If the site was on the Rivière de l'Artibonte, this may have been because the area around the mouth was too swampy for habitation, although this never seemed to be a major concern of the Taíno. The village may also have been located away from the coast for defense from coastal raiders.

The "casa real o palacio" of the chiefdom of Xaraguá, wherein Las Casas says the Adelantado and his company were fed (*Historia*, I:441), was one of a type of very large structures described from other places on Hispaniola and the Caribbean. During the subjugation of the southeastern province of Higüey (about 1500), allegedly in revenge of an ambush of some sailors on the isle of Saona, "they gathered together six or seven hundred men and forced them into a house and there killed them all with knives, and on the orders of the captain, who was, as I have said, a gentleman named Juan de Esquivel, they carried out all of them and lined them up in the plaza of the town so that they could be counted" (II:233).

Similar very large houses were reported by Amerigo Vespucci from the mainland.

> The houses in which they lived were held in common by all, and were so large that each sheltered six hundred people, and eight of them housed ten thousand souls. They were made of the strongest wood, although covered by palm fronds; the shape was like a kind of bell. Every eight years or so they said they moved from one place to another because with the great heat the air was infected, causing great sicknesses. (II:121)

Architecturally, this type of house may have been similar to the one occupied by Behecchio, but from other historical accounts, and from the archaeology of the Taíno settlements of the Greater Antilles, we may infer that on Hispaniola the largest structures were built only for caciques and, along with the plazas which almost always accompanied them, constituted the civic architecture of the settlements. Las Casas expresses this view:

> But the [*caneys*] which were understood by others to be [temples]
> . . . were not temples in the sense that religion or their superstitions
> were practiced there, but were only that the houses of the caciques
> and señores were larger than the rest, and these they called *caneyas*,
> the middle syllable long. I do not know what this term meant, but
> everyone understood that *caney* was the house of the principal
> señor. Some things of religion existed or took place in this house,
> especially the *cohoba* ritual, which were like their sacrifices or ser-
> vices. (Las Casas, *Apologética*, II:680)

The structure in which the Adelantado stayed on his visit to Xaraguá is mentioned again a few years later by Las Casas and is described as "a large and principal house, very elaborate, one of the most beautiful ones which they construct there" (Las Casas, *Historia*, II:236). This account concerns the tragic visit of the *comendador Mayor* Nicholas de Ovando to Xaraguá in 1503. Ovando assassinated eighty of the rulers of the province by barring the doors of Behecchio's *caney* and burning them alive. Thus, in grisly fashion, he gave us an estimate of the building's size (Floyd 1973; Lamb 1956).

"The next day," following Las Casas, "there were in the plaza of the town many other kinds of festivities, and they took Don Bartolomé Colón and the Christians to see them" (*Historia*, I:442). We may suppose that these were further *areyto*s and ceremonies of welcome. From other town descriptions on Hispaniola we can imagine the scene.

> The towns in these islands were not arranged along their streets, except that the house of the king or lord of the town was built in the best place. . . . In front of the palacio there was a large clearing, better swept and smoother, more long than wide, which in the tongue of those islands they call *batey*, . . . which means the ball game.
> There were other houses also near to the plaza, and if the town was a very large one, there were other plazas or courts for the ball game which were of lesser size than the main one. (Las Casas, *Aplogética*, I:121; see also Alegría 1983:8)

Las Casas's narrative of the visit of the Adelantado continued.

> From where they stood among them, there suddenly came out two squads of people armed with their bows and arrows, completely nude, and they started to skirmish and play among themselves, at first just like in Spain, when they play with cañas; little by little things began to heat up, as though they were fighting their worst enemies, and in such a manner they cut themselves, so that in a short time four were dead and many badly hurt. Everyone was rejoicing and peaceful and happy and took no more notice of the injured and dead than if they had been a speck in their eye [un papirote en la cara]. (*Historia*, I:442)

From the rest of the ethnohistorical documents from the period, this display certainly seems not to have been common practice among the Taíno and is not repeated in its ferocity during the conquest period in the islands. Was it an overzealous demonstration of military power? If so, it surely was wasted on the Spaniards, who possessed (and were known to possess) overwhelming technical superiority in such battles. Mock battle with real death was in fact much more a part of the post-Roman and post-Reconquista Spanish cultural repertoire than it was a part of the Taínos'. Was it a reevaluation of death acted out for the Adelantado's benefit? Was it a fabrication on the part of the witnesses, a lie? In the context of Martyr's narrative or Las Casas's it would have served no purpose; neither was inclined to portray the Xaraguáns as militarists. It is an enigma.

The Contract

The business of the Adelantado's visit was transacted that afternoon, when the tribute demands were discussed. Martyr and Las Casas disagree concerning this, Martyr saying, uncertainly, that Behecchio and Bartolomé must have come to an agreement at their first meeting at the Río Neiba. Las Casas gives a more complete account.

> After all of these fiestas and rejoicing, D. Bartolomé Colón spoke to the king Behecchio and this lady, his sister Anacaona, about how his brother the Almirante had been sent by the king and queen of Castille, who were very great kings and lords and had many kingdoms and people under their dominion, and that Colón had returned to Castille to see them and tell them of the many lords and people of this island who were already giving tribute, and of the tribute that they paid, and it was for this reason that the Adelantado had come to him and his kingdom, so that they might see him and be received as lords and in sign of their subservience they might give some tribute. (*Historia*, I:443)

Behecchio's response, well rehearsed probably, since it was not true, was, "How can I give tribute, for in all my kingdom there is no place where gold can be found, nor do my people know what it is?" On the basis of the tribute demands placed on the Vega Real, one-half *cascabel* of gold per vecino every three months, he believed that for the foreigners gold was the only acceptable tribute. But for the Colóns, given the tremendous problem of feeding the Spanish contingent on the island, the value of cassava bread and dried fish was increasing daily. Martyr and Las Casas report a similar response from the Adelantado, as though from the same press release. "We do not want, nor is it our intention to impose a tribute on anyone which they do not possess or know of, but only such things as they have in their lands and can easily pay. Of the things in your province and kingdom that we know to be abundant, such as much cotton and cassava bread, we want what you have the most of, not things that do not exist" (p. 443). This demand was agreed to, Behecchio and Anacaona promising that they and their people would give as much of these sorts of things as the Spaniards wanted.

If this was indeed the way the tribute negotiation took place, with Behecchio and Anacaona together empowered by the other leaders and people of Xaraguá to make such an agreement without consulting anyone else, it is significant for understanding the socio-political organization of the region. The existence of a hierarchy of caciques of varying ranks is implicit in all of the Spanish dealings with the Indians. Las Casas speaks of "Guarionex, Caonabo, Behecchio, and Higuanamá, with all the other infinite kings or minor señores who followed and obeyed them" (I:400). Elsewhere, he gives more detail.

> They have three terms which signified the dignity or station of the
> señores: the first was *guaoxerí*, . . . which was the least of the three
> grades, similar to what we call "caballeros" [gentlemen] or "Vuestra
> Merced" [your grace]; the second was *barbarí*, . . . and this one is
> a higher señor than the first, as when to the señores who have titles we
> call "señoría" [your lordship], they call them *baharí*; the third and
> supreme class was *matunherí*, . . . which were only the supreme
> kings, just as we could call kings "Vuestra Alteza" [your highness],
> they *matunherí* " (Arrom 1975:15)

This three-tiered hierarchy of caciques is often mentioned elsewhere in the chronicles of contact. Whatever the degree of validity it may possess in terms of the cultural categories of the Taíno, this perceived hierarchy was the Spanish model for understanding the political network with which they were dealing. This system, moreover, translated itself into a spatial network of regional, district, and village leaders.

This received system, however, may reflect one of the greatest and most systematic biases in the chronicles as ethnographic documents, for Spanish society, politically and socially, was at the time extremely hierarchical. It is a troubling coincidence that what is now Spain was *itself* divided into four kingdoms—Castille, Ara-

gon, Granada, and Navarre—until the consolidation under Ferdinand and Isabela. The phenomenon of kingship under the newly
emerging nation-states of Europe, of which Spain was the most
powerful, was changing rapidly at this time, but the concept as
it was used by the Colóns, Las Casas, Martyr, and the others
was organized around the medieval and postmedieval principle
of the feudal contract. The king had the qualities of supreme feudal
lord and was the theoretical owner of the land; beneath him was
a dendritic network of vassals, bound in fealty to their superior
partners by the ritual of homage and given an investiture, a symbol
of the right to use the land, by their lords. The vassal provided
the king with military power, with cash or goods when needed,
and with hospitality. The rights and obligations of lords and
vassals were understood by the participants in this feudal contract, as well as by the men who explored the New World.
What the Adelantado offered Behecchio, on behalf of his brother
the Admiral of the Ocean Sea, and in turn on behalf of the
king and queen of Spain, was a corrupt version of the feudal
contract.

If this is what D. Bartolomé Colón offered, how did the cacique
Behecchio understand it? Behecchio's reply certainly surprised Las
Casas, who commented: "Who among the free kings of the world
would submit on the first demand to another king, whom they
had neither seen nor heard, to subject themselves and serve them
as subject and vassal, contrary to natural inclinations?" (*Historia*,
I:443). What Behecchio received, on the one hand, was a personal
reprieve. Being one of what the Spaniards considered a major king
of the island was in 1495 an intensely dangerous position. Of the
four highest ranking caciques mentioned—Guarionex of the Vega
Real, Caonabo of Maguana, Higuanamá of Higüey, and
Behecchio—Caonabo was dead, Guarionex was about to under-
take the half-hearted rebellion that would be his undoing, and
Higuanamá would last only a few years.

On the other hand, there was economic reprieve. Rather than
having to alter radically the economic system of his region by
having to produce a massive amount of gold every three months,
Behecchio was being offered the chance to supply the invaders
with something which was in his power to procure. Finally, he
was reprieved because the Adelantado and his company gave every
indication of being willing to leave if he acceded to their demands.
Instead of being a conquered and occupied territory, he was to

be a reasonably autonomous tributary. There was the prospect at least that a reasonable facsimile of the existing sociopolitical system would survive, providing that the tribute was paid.

Taking the rather unlikely view that Behecchio's conception of the transaction was indeed that of a vassal pledging tribute to a lord misses another possible significance of the event. Texts pertaining to the early contact period of Hawaii portray the Hawaiian's donations of food to the British not as trade or tribute but as sacrifice, as the treatment appropriate to a god (Sahlins 1985:125–25). The analogy may not be out of place here; note the *zemi* ritual that Benzioni (1857) and Gomara (1932) describe, cited above in chapter 3.

Unquestionably, the concepts that the Adelantado was presenting were not at all those which Behecchio may have been receiving. The meaning of gifts was undoubtedly different in the two cultures, as were the meanings of dominance and subjugation, of elites and nonelites, or of hosts and guests. There is also the problem of relying on the questionable ethnographic capabilities of the Spanish and Italian observers.

But to take the culturally relativistic view that what was occurring in the negotiations between members of these two cultural systems was a sort of shadow dance, in which neither could comprehend the intentions and motivations of the other, is to miss one of the most fascinating observations about the contact period between the Old World and the New. The cultural traditions of the Taíno and the Spanish had developed independently, in complete isolation from one another, for more than twenty thousand years prior to their resumption of interaction in 1492. As nearly as is known, the complex social and political inventions of the two groups emerged in isolation. Yet in the set of interactions we can observe between Behecchio and Bartolomé, and throughout the conquest history of the New World, there is a remarkable degree of real conceptual understanding and commonality of purpose. The ways in which the problems of relatively large, sedentary, agricultural populations had been accommodated in the two societies were not so different that effective social and political discourse was impossible.

The narrative of this set of interactions ends here for Martyr and Las Casas. The Adelantado and his company left overland. "After having advised the cacique to henceforth plant more cotton along the river banks, the Adelantado left on the third day for

Isabela to visit the invalids and to see the ships in construction" (Martyr 1970:120). With the disappointing arrival of the caravels in July and with no immediate prospect of the arrival of help from Spain, the Adelantado's task was to maintain the dispersed settlements on the island, to counter the increasingly militaristic forces of Guarionex and his allies in the Vega Real, and to control unrest among the anti-Colón factions among the Spaniards (an almost hopeless undertaking by this point).

The Spirit of the Gift

The story of the encounter with the Spanish forces in Xaraguá resumes several months later, late in the year 1496 or early 1497, when the Adelantado received word from Behecchio that the tribute was prepared. His reason for going so quickly to collect a tribute of cotton, for which there was no immediate need or use, was the continuing problem of feeding his army. Las Casas comments that they went to Xaraguá "to go and find food in such land that had not been worked over like the Christians had done La Vega and its territories" (*Historia*, I:447). By this time a large number of Spaniards, "desperados" in Las Casas's view, had renounced the Colón family's leadership and either had aligned themselves with Francisco Roldán, the leader of the Colóns' opposition, or had established themselves in villages throughout the Vega Real.

The hospitality the Adelantado received on his second trip to Xaraguá was similar to his first. Behecchio and Anacaona and the thirty-two principal señores came out and met them on the road, a feast was prepared, and the tribute of cotton was presented. "Thirty-two caciques," says Martyr, "were assembled in the house of Anacauchoa, where they had brought their tribute. In addition to what had been agreed upon, they sought to win favour by adding numerous presents, which consisted of two kinds of bread, roots, grains, utias, . . . fish, . . . and those same serpents, resembling crocodiles, which they esteem a most delicate food" (1970:123). This was hospitality appreciated, without doubt. Bartolomé sent word overland to Isabela for one of the completed caravels to be brought around the northwest coast of Hispaniola, a sea voyage of slightly under 480 km (300 mi) with the wind and current behind them most of the way. Their time in Xaraguá, waiting for this return, was apparently without incident, and in contrast to the primitive conditions in the mining regions or in the upset Vega Real, it was undoubtedly a pleasant stay.

When the news arrived that the caravel was at the harbor, 10 km (6 mi) from the village, Anacaona is said to have persuaded Behecchio and the people to accompany the Spaniards to the ship and to stop midway for the night. As Las Casas describes it, "Anacaona had a little hamlet [lugarejo] halfway along the road, where they wished to spend that night. There this lady had a house full of a thousand things made of cotton, and seats and many vessels and things of service in the house, made of wood, marvelously worked, and it was this place and house where they rested" (*Historia*, I:447).

This incident suggests another layer of complexity for the woman Anacaona, already an enigmatic personality, as well as another dimension to the general category of exchange among the Taíno. Sister to Behecchio and apparently an equal partner in the negotiations with the Adelantado, wife to Caonabo and perhaps his successor as cacique of Maguana, Anacaona also possesses a hamlet within the cacicazgo of Xaraguá and keeps there a storehouse of the most valuable of Taíno prestige goods. Las Casas continued:

> The Lady presented Don Bartolomé with many of these seats, the most beautiful, which were all black and polished as if they were of *azavaja*; and offered all the other things which were for table service (and naguas of cotton, which were like little skirts carried by the women from the waist to midleg, woven of the same cotton, white and marvelous) and it pleased them for him to take whatever he would. They gave him four large balls of spun cotton so large that it pained a man to lift them. (P. 447)

This is a transaction apart from the delivery of tribute. That had already been done at the village of Behecchio and had exceeded the expectations of the Spaniards.

The importance of the exchange of prestige goods among the Taíno is suggested both archaeologically and historically. This system seems to be intimately and intricately involved in the signification and distribution of power and connected in complex ways with the process of elite intermarriage and the ball game mentioned above.

In understanding this prestige good system we are drawn back to the problem of Anacaona's status and marriage, for among the Taíno, as with many societies woven together by the relations of hierarchically ranked lineages, the movement of high-status prestige goods is linked to the movement of high-ranking spouses from lineage to lineage. In the Spaniard's calculus of social and political rank, Xaraguá was superior to Maguana, the cacicazgo of Caonabo. Assuming for the moment that this is correct, that in this marriage the wife givers outranked the wife takers, we are left with no concrete suggestion of the exchange relationship between the polities. It could be that Anacaona, arguably the highest-ranking woman in Xaraguá, was unmarriageable within the society. This would present a situation like that on Samoa, where the sister of a paramount chief would be of equal or superior rank to her brother and thus would remain a sacred virgin unless an appropriate off-island marriage could be arranged (Friedman 1982:187).

Further inconsistencies prevent a clear and simple reconstruction of the prestige good system and its ramifications in the kinship and political relations of the Taíno. The view of the cacique as omnipotent in social, political, and economic spheres is not supported. It was Anacaona who gave prestige goods to the Adelantado, not Behecchio. Moreover, in the context of Anacaona's gift of high-status objects, the Spaniards understood the following:

> It is in the manufacture of these articles [carved objects of *Lignum vitae*, a dense black wood] that the islanders devote the best of their native ingenuity. In the island of Ganabara [Ile de la Gonâve, in the bay before Port-au-Prince] which . . . lies at the western extremity of Hispaniola and which is subject to Anacauchoa, it is the women who are thus employed. (Martyr 1970:125)

As noted above, the qualities of the social and political statuses passed through matrilines and patrilines are not known, nor is it known exactly what statuses or offices individual men or women held, but in this case the gift of prestige goods was within the purview of Anacaona, and the ability to manufacture these high-status goods was a quality of women.

As the company arrived at the bay of Port-au-Prince in the Gulf of Gonâve, there is another indication of Anacaona's status. According to Las Casas, "The king and the queen, his sister, each had canoes, very large and well painted and prepared, but the lady, being so regal [palaciana], did not want to go in the canoe, but only with Don Bartolomé in the boat" (*Historia*, I:448). Martyr differs slightly, saying that "the king also commanded two canoes to be launched, the first for the use of himself and his attendants, and the second for his sister and her followers" (Martyr 1970:126). He also adds that at the coast there was a third "royal town" (p. 126).

Throughout the ethnohistory of the Caribbean, large and elaborate canoes are an important symbol of rank. The largest would hold 50 to 150 people (McKusick 1960). Coasting northern Cuba, the Admiral saw several such canoes. Because these vessels represented the status of caciques when meeting other dignitaries away from their villages, Colón, who was loath to leave his own ship, saw many of them in the Lesser and Greater Antilles.

The Spaniards then had the opportunity to show off for the Xaraguáns.

> Arriving close to the caravel, some lombards were fired, terrifying the kings and their many servants and attendants [privados] to such a degree that it appeared to them that the sky was falling, and they threw themselves into the water; but when they saw Don Bartolomé laughing, they recovered somewhat [algo se asosegaron]. They arrived, as mariners say, on board, on the caravel, the sailors began to play a tambourine and a flute and other instruments that they had, and it was a marvel to see how they cheered up. (*Historia*, I:448)

The anchor was raised and the ship sailed around a bit, apparently dumbfounding Behecchio and Anacaona. "Here I don't think they feared anything . . . , they stood without fear in quiet admiration that without oars or paddles the caravel, so huge, would go where they wanted, and with a wind only coming from one direction that they could turn against it" (p. 448). Martyr says that "their astonishment [was] so profound that they had nothing to say" (1970:126).

Epilogue

The story of the Spanish in Xaraguá, while it was still a functioning cacicazgo with indigenous leaders at least, ends six years later with a series of confused accounts of the death of Anacaona and many of the other caciques.

Through the turn of the century there was a growing realization in Spain that the colonies of Hispaniola were growing less and less under the control of the crown. The Colón family had never so much ruled as struggled to hold together the diverse and undisciplined factions of the first decade of exploration and conquest. Ferdinand sought a strong ruler to subjugate the colonists and represent his interests. Francisco de Bobadilla had been sent by Isabela to investigate the many charges against the Colón family, and while bringing a greater measure of order to the island than had existed previously, he was still unable to satisfy the crown with the collection of the "royal fifth."

Nicolás de Ovando, a noble of the order of Alcántara, was sent to Hispaniola in the spring of 1502. He ordered Bobadilla, Francisco Roldán, and several of his followers off to Spain to answer the charges of Colón, now somewhat returned to favor and away on his fourth and last voyage, but both died in a hurricane between Hispaniola and Puerto Rico (giving Colón material with which to speculate on the nature of divine justice).

On Hispaniola, Ovando reorganized the island, emphasizing the need to establish large areas of food production to supply the mines. These included the Vega Real, Higüey, and Xaraguá. The province of Higüey, encompassing most of the southeastern corner of the island, was brutally put down by Juan de Esquivel, who, as mentioned above, had six to seven hundred bodies dragged from the *caney* into the plaza to be counted. Ovando then turned his attention to the west, to Xaraguá, which had enjoyed relatively good relations with Spaniards but which had been a haven for renegades since the visits of the Adelantado in 1496 and 1497. Here Ovando's task was not to suppress an indigenous rebellion but to subjugate a somewhat separatist community of both Spaniards and Taíno. Floyd (1973:60) estimates that there were over one hundred Spaniards living in the region, a collection of former followers of Roldán and people who had jumped ship to stay in the relative paradise of Xaraguá.

Ovando took three hundred men and an unspecified contingent of Indians into Xaraguá and received much the same regal welcome as had the Adelantado. Ovando was housed in the same *caney* as the Adelantado had been, and Anacaona "ordered all of the señores of that kingdom and all the people of their towns to come to her city of Xaraguá to receive, celebrate, and give their reverence to the *Guamiquina* of the Christians" (Las Casas, *Historia*, II:236). Despite a continual Spanish presence, the upper stratum of the Xaraguán sociopolitical structure seemed intact.

Behecchio had died in the interim, and Martyr reports that Anacaona, as was their custom, "caused to be buried alive with her brother the most beautiful of his wives or concubines, Guanahattabenecheuá; and she would have buried others but for the intercession of a . . . Franciscan friar" (Martyr 1970:387). Barlow and many others report the same practice.

> And when eny of the gret men of the indies which be called caciques die, thei make a gret hole in th ground wherin thei put him setting and sett before him both mete and drinke and so cover the hole ageine wᵗ tymbres and turves of earthe upon it, and leve open a hole as bigge as one maie scant go in at and then as many of his wyfes as do ernestlie love him take mete with them and goeth into the hole, and after thei be in thei cover the hole wᵗ tymbre and erthe so that thei can come no more owt ageyne, and thei have a belefe and saie thei go to acompany him to an other worlde when thei shal have more honor and pleasure then thei have here. (Barlow 1832:168)

Las Casas (*Historia*, II:236–39), Antonio de Herrera y Tordisillas (*Historia*, I:140–43), and others offer partial and conflicting accounts of Ovando's visit. Ultimately however, through a rather dubious ploy, eighty caciques (but cf. Floyd 1973:242, n. 20) were lured into the *caney* of the paramount chief of Xaraguá and burned alive. "As for the queen and Lady Anacaona, in order to show her honor, they hung her" (Las Casas, *Historia*, II:238).

The portrayal of this event as a Spanish suppression of a real or potential Indian revolt is questioned by Pérez de Tudela (1955:378–79), Lamb (1956:126), and Floyd (1973:60–64). These authors envision the incident as the subjugation of a Spanish-Xaraguán alliance of caciques and renegades who, for their mutual benefit, had been evading demands from Santo Domingo for food and laborers to work in the mines. Fifty Spaniards were killed in the battle, an impossible number if it were such a rout as the official version, which Herrera and Las Casas describe (Floyd 1973:62). Xaraguá was the last of the pre-Hispanic cacicazgos on Hispaniola to be destroyed.

5

∗∗∗∗∗∗

Conclusions

From 1492 into the 1520s, Hispaniola was the scene of one of the most dramatic encounters in human history. Two human groups that had been separated by tens of millennia—since Upper Palaeolithic people crossed the Bering land bridge and colonized the New World—rediscovered each other through the voyages of discovery of the newly formed nation-state of Spain. For the first few years, the Spanish venture was a small and rather tentative affair, beset with problems and unprofitable. In the course of those first years, however, the Spaniards adapted and refined many of the concepts and methods that they would use in the colonization of the rest of the New World—concepts for understanding New World peoples and their cultures, and methods for exploiting the new territories for European profit.

In social and demographic terms the contact period on Hispaniola was a monumental catastrophe. When the Spanish forces moved westward onto the Mexican mainland, as conquistadores rather than discoverers, they left a Taíno population on Hispaniola of a few hundred or thousand, where twenty years before the island's inhabitants numbered more than a million (Cook and Borah 1971; cf. Rosenblat 1967). Those few remaining did not survive for long.

Disease appears to have been the primary agent in the decimation of Hispaniola's population. Europe had for centuries been a center for trade with all parts of the Old World, and through a long series of epidemics and plagues, its people had acquired immunity to a multitude of diseases (LeRoy Ladurie 1981). They carried these diseases with them to the New World and exposed them to populations which had no immunity.

135

This fundamental cause of the annihilation of Hispaniola's people was exacerbated by several other factors. The Spanish presence put additional stress on the Taíno economic system; from the beginning the foreigners consumed a great deal of food (chapter 3). In a manioc-based horticultural economy, in which plants take up to a year to mature, very little surplus of harvested and prepared food was available (Sturdevant 1961; Roosevelt 1980). The manioc remained in the ground until it was needed. When an army of Spaniards and Indian camp followers descended upon a village, all of the manioc may have been harvested, even that which would not have been mature for six months to a year (Wilson 1985b). When the food resources were exhausted and the army moved on, the manioc cycle of the village was completely disrupted. The villagers had to harvest the remaining plants to survive, and by doing so, ensured a famine in the months to come.

The horticultural system also suffered from the population displacement the foreigners brought about. The Spanish presence brought large groups of people together for a variety of reasons. During Colón's first voyage he was met at every anchorage by multitudes of people on shore who had come to trade or merely to see the strangers (chapter 2). Hundreds, perhaps thousands, of Indians followed Colón's army as it marched into the Vega Real during the second voyage. The wars of rebellion in the Vega Real brought many thousands of people together, and more often, the threatening Spanish presence caused people to flee their homes and crops for the safety of other villages or the mountains (chapter 3). When a system of forced labor was instituted and people had to leave their villages for several months to work in the gold mines, additional problems were created in supplying food for the mining camps, as well as in the villages they had left (Arranz Márquez 1979; Sued Badillo 1983; Zabala 1949). All of these incidents of population displacement put stress on a horticultural system that was based on minimal surplus and continual maintenance. Just as they could not stand to be completely harvested at one time, the manioc gardens could not be left unattended indefinitely. While disease probably accounted for the majority of deaths, after 1495 starvation was constantly present as a contributing factor.

In a way somewhat parallel to the delicately balanced horticultural system, the indigenous sociopolitical system was subject to intense disturbances brought about by the presence of the Spaniards. From the glimpses of the interactions among the elite stratum of Taíno society presented in chapters 2–4, it appears that the modes of interaction between elites were structured, as they are in all hierarchical societies, by a complex set of principles. The relations of the members of the Taíno elite, especially high-ranking caciques, were ordered in ways that would avoid uncontrolled or unnecessary conflict. During the contact period the Taíno elite were uncertain about where the foreigners should be treated in the indigenous system of social and political ranking: Were they equivalent to commoners, elites, or gods? Especially in the events surrounding the uprisings of confederated polities in the Vega Real (chapter 3), this uncertainty seems to have thrown relations among the indigenous elite out of balance, causing enough division among Taíno leaders that their attempts at coordinated military resistance were impaired.

The principal goal of this book has been to offer a descriptive reconstruction of Taíno culture during the period of European contact, with special emphasis on social and political organization. The Taíno of the Greater Antilles are significant not just because they were the first group subjected to European colonization. The complex Taíno society emerged in relative isolation from the rest of the New World peoples that was imposed by distance and ocean travel and did so in the unique environment of the Caribbean archipelago. They addressed problems of sea travel and trade and transplanted modes of production adapted to the tropical forests into the many and diverse ecosystems of the Caribbean islands. In the process, they developed a form of sociopolitical organization that is structurally similar to that of other hierarchical societies in the New World, and yet unique to the Caribbean.

In the narrative descriptions which compose this book, a secondary theme has been to examine some of the mechanisms which played a part in changing and elaborating the Taíno's complex sociopolitical institutions. Because of the limitations of the evidence—the documents are incomplete and cover a very few years—this study cannot hope to explain adequately the emergence of these Taíno institutions. However, the ethnohistorical documents record patterns of interaction among the Taíno elite which provide insight into the historical mechanisms through which the Taíno chiefdoms became larger, more inclusive, and structurally more complex. Examining these mechanisms and attempting to understand their potential impact on the structure of Taíno society is a necessary step in constructing a satisfactory explanation of the historical emergence of these societies. At best, however, it is only a part of the intellectual process of understanding the development of the Caribbean chiefdoms. Our knowledge of the political, economic, and demographic trajectories which resulted in the contact-period societies discussed here is still incomplete.

It is clear that the societies of the Greater Antilles encountered by the Spaniards had changed remarkably from the Lesser Antillean societies of the first five hundred years A.D. (Alcina Franch 1983; Keegan 1985; Rouse 1985; Rouse and Allaire 1978). While the latter possessed hierarchies of social status, a ritual and ceremonial repertoire, and a system of long-distance trade in prestige goods, the larger-scale, more complex sociopolitical institutions of the Taíno had emerged and flourished in the centuries following the colonization of the Greater Antilles. The ethnohistorical documents of the Spaniards suggest that this florescence was continuing until the cataclysmic destruction of the Taíno (Wilson 1985a).

Leaving aside for the moment the questions concerning the nature of this development and its ultimate causes, it is argued here that some of the important changes that accompanied this development—factors which were closely involved with the development of the institutions of complex chiefdoms—involved the concentration of social status and political authority into fewer and fewer lineages. Simultaneously, a greater importance came to be attached to these dimensions of social and political status, making them more valuable for individuals to possess and thus more urgently desired. The concomitants of this were fundamental changes in the social organization of Taíno society.

In examining the factors leading to the consolidation of elite status and political power into a few descent lines, some aspects of the Taíno kinship system have continually frustrated any attempt to be clearly understood. The nature of inheritance and succession patterns—in particular, the inheritance of individual qualities through both matriline and patriline—confounds the attempt to understand the Taíno kinship system completely (Cassá 1974; Helms 1980; Keegan and Maclachlan 1989; Sued Badillo 1985). Yet in some respects these considerations are the most crucial for understanding changes in sociopolitical structure. I believe that the inheritance and succession rules are so difficult to codify precisely because they were so important in the competition for social status and political power. In a highly competitive arena, the principles of succession and inheritance may have been contested, reinterpreted, and transformed in cases where some of the individuals involved would have benefited (Comaroff 1978).

The marriage of elite members of different polities produced far-reaching changes in the sociopolitical structure of Taíno society. The practice of exogamous marriage (i.e. occurring across cacicazgos) by high-ranking people seems to have been a central mechanism in the consolidation of smaller polities into larger ones, first in the creation of multivillage alliances, and then in the incorporation of several of these multivillage units into cacicazgos like Behecchio and Anacaona's Xaraguá, Caonabo's Maguana, or Guarionex's Magua.

One way in which the intermarriage of elites may have resulted in the merging of two political units is through dual succession, in which an individual could inherit high-status roles in two cacicazgos. The practice hinges on a measure of ambiguity about the preferred heir. Potentially, an inheriting cacique could succeed his mother's brother, and in some instances could succeed his own father as well. As discussed in chapter 4, these rules were apparently rather fluid, and in practice, succession decisions probably depended to an extent on acquired statuses as well as inherited ones—and on the political maneuvering of the people involved. It appears that a child of the union of Anacaona and Caonabo would possess the necessary hereditary qualifications to be a cacique in either cacicazgo, or both.

A significant outcome of the practice of elite intermarriage was the creation of overarching kinship ties which connected the elite strata of the various Taíno cacicazgos. Exogamous marriages among the Taíno elite linked large-scale descent groups and disrupted the prior pattern of ranked or "conical" descent groups (Keegan and Maclachlan 1989; Loven 1935; Rouse 1948). Instead of merging the two conical structures, however, and recalculating their implied social ranking, this process appears to have been leading to a fundamental disjunction between commoner and elite lineages. The results of this process, if this reconstruction is accurate, were not fully realized among the Taíno; clear social stratification never emerged in the pre-Hispanic Caribbean (Alcina Franch 1983; Cassá 1974, 1984). That some lineages possessed higher status than others is clear, however, and the existence of an elite lineage which linked polities and even islands seems clear.

Another trend that is significant for understanding sociopolitical change among the Taíno is the practice of polygyny among caciques in major cacicazgos. The chroniclers were clearly intrigued and often commented on the practice. The comments, unfortunately, were quantitative rather than interpretive (Behecchio had thirty wives, it is always noted). As noted in the discussion of Anacaona, the woman of Xaraguá, some aspects of political status were transmitted from mother to son or mother to daughter but held by men. For example, most of the documents pertaining to succession mention that a cacique's sister's son was a preferred heir. As cacicazgos became larger and caciques managed to extract from them greater quantities of food and labor, a large number of wives became an affordable display of status (and a valuable political asset). Archaeologically, it appears that practices on such a scale were unusual or unknown before the migration of the Arawak speakers into the Greater Antilles (Rouse 1982; Sanoja Obediente 1983; Sued Badillo 1979).

Since essential qualities of social and political status were carried through matrilines, the practic of polygyny on a large scale by caciques would tend to concentrate such high-status qualities into a single descent line. A powerful cacique thus appropriates not only the products of subordinate polities but their high-ranking lineages as well. The multiple names of caciques is suggestive in this regard: "Whenever Beuchios [Las Casas: Behecchio] . . . publishes an order, or makes his wishes known by heralds' proclamation, he takes great care to have [his five] names and forty more recited" (Martyr 1970:387).

A more direct practice also led to the consolidation of the Taíno chiefdoms. As noted in chapter Four, Las Casas was told that a cacique could in effect ally or deed his cacicazgo to another, more powerful cacique, in order to gain protection from other competitors. In some cases, the subordinate cacique may in fact be heir to the superior cacique, making his diminished status and political power a temporary one.

On the basis of archaeological evidence, it is evident that over a period of centuries sociopolitical complexity increased in the Caribbean (Allaire 1973; Rouse and Allaire 1978). Village size and populations grew, the trade in prestige goods became widespread and elaborate, and political units became fewer and larger. Over shorter time periods, however, it is unimaginable that there were not countervailing trends to the ones discussed here. If the concentration of high-status descent lines led to political consolidation and social stratification, there were undoubtedly forces which disrupted or negated these trends. The ethnohistorical documents, however, do not speak directly to these counterforces. Dissent, revolt, the failure of a descent line without acceptable heirs, conquest, assassination, or any number of other circumstances would disrupt the processes argued for here. Yet in a documentary record which for our purposes is less than a decade in length, they do not appear. Such forces almost certainly existed, however. It may be that such centrifugal forces did not fall within the chaotic years of the conquest, or that the disruption of the presence of the Europeans submerged them beneath more pressing concerns. Alternatively, it is possible that such events and forces were not understandable or interpretable from the Spaniard's perspective and hence were not recorded by them.

The survival of a polity in a social environment of other competing cacicazgos depended on a range of activities apart from astute marriage alliances. Warfare between cacicazgos, both in the sense of conquest (consolidation of political units by force) and in the highly stylized form of the ball game, was one. Coupled with the ball game was the practice of feast giving, a reciprocal and competitive exchange between cacicazgos which, in part, established a cacique's place in relation to other caciques and facilitated other projects such as marriage alliances and the trading of prestige goods.

The exchange of prestige goods that surrounded the Adelantado's visit to Xaraguá suggests the central importance of such transactions among the Taíno elite. Symbols of high rank such as the carved *Lignum vitae* stools, or *dujos*, were apparently tied to chiefly status, but potent objects like the personal *zemis* or the "black *turey* of Viscaya" and esoteric knowledge (Helms 1979), like the *areyto* which Guarionex gave to Mayobanex and his people, were also critical requisites of social and political status (chapter Three).

A fascinating and still unclear aspect of the Taíno system of prestige goods concerns the role of women as the producers and givers of some of the most powerful of these gifts. With this observation, the problems of the kinship patterns of the Taíno elite are immediately reopened, but with no new resolution suggested.

Hispaniola was the first foothold in the European conquest and colonization of the New World. Before the Spaniards' attention was turned to Puerto Rico, Cuba, and the coasts of Central and South America in the early sixteenth century, it was the only European base of operations. In the years between 1492 and the *repartimiento* of 1514, the population of Hispaniola had declined from a figure very likely in the millions (Henige 1978a, 1978b; Cook and Borah 1971; Zambardino 1978; cf. Rosenblat 1967), to around thirty thousand (Henige 1978a:231). By the 1540s, only a few of the original inhabitants could be found (Cook and Borah 1971).

What happened on Hispaniola provides a metaphor for the subsequent history of the contact period in the New World. We may see the same themes of understanding and misunderstanding, greed and generosity, humanity and inhumanity acted out again and again in the subsequent centuries, and lasting to the present day. But on Hispaniola the impact of the discovery of the New World by the Old was more concentrated in time and space and was as completely devastating for the aboriginal inhabitants as in any other place in the New World.

****

Bibliography

Alcina Franch, José
   1983. "La cultura taína como sociedad de transición entre los niveles tribal y de jefaturas." In *La cultura taína*, 69–80. Madrid: Comisión Nacional para la Celebración del V Centenario del Descubrimiento de América.
Alegría, Ricardo E.
   1951. "The Ball Game Played by the Aborigines of the Antilles." *American Antiquity* 16(4): 348–52.
   1965. "Caribbean Symposium: On Puerto Rican Archaeology." *American Antiquity* 31(2):246–49.
   1976. "Las relaciones entre los Taínos de Puerto Rico y los de la Española." *Boletín del Instituto Montecristeño de Arqueología* no. 2.
   1978. *Apuntes en torno a la mitología de los Indios Taínos de las Antillas Mayores y sus orígenes suramericanos.* Santo Domingo: Museo del Hombre Dominicano.
   1979. "Apuntes para el estudio de los caciques de Puerto Rico." *Revista del Instituto de Cultura Puertorriqueña* 85:25–41.
   1980. *El tesoro de los Indios Taínos de la Española y Cristóbal Colón.* Santo Domingo, Dominican Republic: Fundación García Arévalo.
   1983. *Ball Courts and Ceremonial Plazas in the West Indies.* New Haven: Yale University Publications in Anthropology, no. 79.
Allaire, Louis
   1973. *Vers une préhistoire des Petites Antilles.* Ste-Marie, Martinique: Centre de Recherches Caraibes de l'Université de Montréal.
   1974. "An Archaeological Reconnaissance of St. Kitts, Leeward Islands." *Proceedings of the Fifth International Congress for the Study of Pre-Columbian Cultures of the Lesser Antilles,* 158–61.

1977. "Later Prehistory in Martinique and the Island Caribs: Problems in Ethnic Identification." Ph.D. diss. Yale University.

1980. "On the Historicity of Carib Migrations in the Lesser Antilles." *American Antiquity* 45(2): 238–45.

1984. "A Reconstruction of Early Historical Island Carib Pottery." *Southeastern Archaeology* 3(2): 121–33.

1988. "Volcanism and the Early Saladoid Occupation of Martinique." Paper presented at the fifty-third annual meeting of the Society for American Archaeology, Phoenix, Arizona, April 27–May 1.

Alvarado Zayas, Pedro A.
1981. "La cerámica del centro ceremonial de tibes: Estudio descriptivo." Master's thesis, Centro de Estudios Avanzados de Puerto Rico y El Caribe, San Juan.

Archivo General de Indias, Sevilla
1517. *Interrogatorio jeronimiano de 1517.* Sección Indiferente, legajo 1624.

Armstrong, Douglas V.
1978. "Archaic Shellfish Gatherers of St. Kitts, Leeward Islands: A Case Study in Subsistence and Settlement Patterns." Master's thesis, University of California, Los Angeles.

1979. "'Scrap' or Tools: A Closer Look at *Strombus gigas* Columella Artifacts." *Journal of the Virgin Islands Archaeological Society* 7:27–34.

Arnáiz, P. Fco. José
1983. "El mundo religioso taíno visto por la fe católica española." In *La cultura taína,* 141–54. Madrid: Comisión Nacional para la Celebración del V Centenario del Descubrimiento de América.

Arranz Márquez, Luis
1979. *Emigración española a Indias: Poblamiento y despoblación antillanos.* Santo Domingo: Fundación García Arévalo.

Arrom, José Juan
1967. *El mundo mítico de los Taínos.* Bogotá: Instituto Caro y Cuervo.

1971. "El mundo mítico de los Taínos: Notas sobre el ser supremo." *Revista Dominicana de Arqueología y Antropología* 1(1): 71–73.

1975. *Mitología y artes prehispánicas de las Antillas.* Mexico City: Siglo XXI Editores.

Ballesteros y Beretta, Antonio
1945. *Cristóbal Colón y el descubrimiento de América.* Barcelona: Salvat Editores. (Vols. 4 and 5 of *Historia de América y de los pueblos americanos*)

Barlow, Roger
1832. *A Brief Summe of Geographie.* London: Hakluyt Society.

Beaglehole, J. C.
   1967. *The Journals of Captain James Cook on His Voyages of Discovery.* Vol. 3: *The Voyage of the "Resolution" and "Discovery," 1776–1780.* Cambridge: Cambridge University Press.
Bécher, A. B.
   1856. *The Landfall of Columbus on His First Voyage to America.* London: J. D. Potter.
Benzioni, Girolamo
   1857. *History of the New World.* Translated by W. H. Smyth. London: Hakluyt Society.
Blume, Helmut
   1974. *The Caribbean Islands.* London: Longman Group.
Boomert, Aad
   1978. "Pre-Columbian Raised Fields in Coastal Surinam." *Proceedings of the Eighth International Congress for the Study of Pre-Columbian Cultures of the Lesser Antilles,* 134–44.
   1983. "The Saladoid Occupation of Wonotobo Falls, Western Surinam." *Proceedings of the Ninth International Congress for the Study of Pre-Columbian Cultures of the Lesser Antilles,* 97–120.
   1985. "The Cayo Complex of St. Vincent and Its Mainland Origin." Paper presented at the Eleventh International Congress for Caribbean Archaeology, San Juan, Puerto Rico, June 28–July 3.
Bourne, Edward G.
   1906. "Ramón Pané: Treatise on the Antiquities of the Indians of Haiti, Which He as One Who Knows Their Language Diligently Collected by the Command of the Admiral [Christopher Columbus]." *American Antiquarian Society Proceedings* 17:318–38.
Boyrie de Moya, Emile de
   1960. "Cinco años de arqueología dominicana." *Revista Anales* 26(93–96): 23–98.
Bradstreet, Theodore E., and Alfredo E. Figueredo
   1974. "Ceramic Culture Site Location Parameters for the Virgin Islands." Paper presented at the thirty-ninth annual meeting of the Society for American Archaeology.
Brau, Salvador
   1966. *La colonización de Puerto Rico.* San Juan, P.R.:Instituto de Cultura Puertorriqueña.
Braudel, Fernand
   1972–74. *The Mediterranean and the Mediterranean World in the Age of Phillip II.* 2 vols. Translated by Siân Reynolds. New York: Harper and Row.
   1980. *On History.* Translated by Sarah Matthews. Chicago: University of Chicago Press.

1982–84. *Civilization and Capitalism, Fifteenth–Eighteenth Century.* Vol. 1: *The Perspective of the World;* vol. 2: *The Structures of Everyday Life;* vol. 3: *The Wheels of Commerce.* Translated by Siân Reynolds. New York: Harper and Row.

Brochado, J. P.
1984. "An Ecological Model of the Spread of Pottery and Agriculture into Eastern South America." Ph.D. diss., University of Illinois, Urbana.

Bullen, Ripley P.
1964. "The Archaeology of Grenada, West Indies." *Contributions of the Florida State Museum, Social Sciences,* 11.

Bullen, Ripley P., and Adelaide K. Bullen
1979. "Settlement Pattern and Environment in Columbian Eastern Dominican Republic." *Boletín del Museo del Hombre Dominicano* 12:315–23.

Callaghan, R. T.
1985. "Pre-ceramic Connections between Central America and the Greater Antilles." Paper presented at the Eleventh Meeting of the International Association for Caribbean Archaeology, San Juan, Puerto Rico.

Campbell, Donald T.
1969. "Ethnocentrism of Disciplines and the Fish-Scale Model of Omniscience." In *Interdisciplinary Relationships in the Social Sciences,* edited by Muzafer Sherif and Carolyn W. Sherif, 328–84. Chicago: Aldine.

Carneiro, Robert L.
1970. "A Theory of the Origin of the State." *Science* 169:733–38.
1983. "The Chiefdom: Precursor of the State," In *The Transition to Statehood in the New World,* edited by Grant Jones and Robert R. Kautz, 37–75. Cambridge: Cambridge University Press.

Cassá, Roberto
1974. *Los Taínos de la Española.* Santo Domingo, Dominican Republic: Editora de la Universidad Autónoma de Santo Domingo.
1984. *Historia social y económica de la República Dominicana.* Vol. 1. Santo Domingo: Punto y Aparte, Editores.

Chanca, Diego Alverez
1932. *Letter to the City of Sevilla.* Translated by Cecil Jane. London: Hakluyt Society.

Chanlatte Baik, Luis A.
1976. *La hueca y sorcé (Vieques, Puerto Rico): Nuevo esquema para los procesos culturales de la arqueología antillana.* Santo Domingo: Fundación García Arévalo.
1985. *Arqueología de Guayanilla y Vieques.* Rio Piedras, P.R.: Centro de Investigaciones Arqueológicas, Universidad de Puerto Rico.

Charlevoix, Pierre François de
1731–33. *Histoire de l'Isle Espagnole ou de S. Domingue.* Paris: Chez François Barois.
Clerc, Edgar
1968. "Sites precolombiens de la Grande-Terre de la Guadaloupe." *Proceedings of the Second International Congress for the Study of Pre-Columbian Cultures of the Lesser Antilles,* 47–60.
Coe, William R., II
1957. "A Distinctive Artifact Common to Haiti and Central America." *American Antiquity* 22:280–82.
Colección de documentos inéditos
1864–84. *Colección de documentos inéditos relativos al descubrimiento . . . de las antiquas posesiones españolas de América y Oceania.* 42 vols. Madrid.
Columbus, Christopher
1893. "Journal of the First Voyage of Columbus." In *The Journal of Christopher Columbus (during His First Voyage, 1492–1493), and Documents Relating to the Voyages of John Cabot and Gaspar Corte Real,* translated by Clements R. Markham, 15–196. London: Hakluyt Society.
Columbus, Don Ferdinand
1824. "History of the Discovery of America, by Christopher Columbus, Written by His Son Don Ferdinand Columbus." In *A General History and Collection of Voyages and Travels,* vol. 3, edited by Robert Kerr, 1–339. Edinburgh: William Blackwood.
Comaroff, John L.
1978. "Rules and Rulers: Political Processes in a Tswana Chiefdom." *Man* 13:1–20.
Cook, S. F., and W. Borah
1971. "The Aboriginal Population of Hispaniola." In *Essays in Population History,* vol 1: *Mexico and the Caribbean,* edited by S. F. Cook and W. Borah, 376–410. Berkeley: University of California Press.
Cornilliac, J. J.
1875. "Anthropologie des Antilles," *Compte-rendu du Congress International des Americanists, Première Session* 2:148–68.
Creamer, W., and J. Haas
1985. "Tribes vs. Chiefdoms in Lower Central America." *American Antiquity* 50:738–54.
Cuneo, Michele de
1893. "Lettera de Michele de Cuneo a Nobili Domino Hieronymo Annari (Savona, 15–28 Ottobre 1495)." In *Raccolta di Documenti e Studi,* 95–107. Rome: R. Commissione Colombiana pel Quarto Centenario Dalla Scoperta Dell'America, part 3, vol 2.

Davis, David D.
    N.d. "Island Carib Origins: Evidence and Non-evidence." Unpublished manuscript.
    1982. "Archaic Settlement and Resource Exploitation in the Lesser Antilles: Preliminary Information from Antigua." *Caribbean Journal of Science* 17:107–22.
De Vorsey, Louis, Jr., and John Parker
    1985. *In the Wake of Columbus: Islands and Controversy.* Detroit: Wayne State University Press.
Deagan, Kathleen A.
    1985. "Spanish-Indian Interaction in Sixteenth-Century Florida and Hispaniola." In *Cultures in Contact*, edited by William W. Fitzhugh, 281–318. Washington, D.C.: Smithsonian Institution Press.
    1987. "Initial Encounters: Arawak Responses to European Contact at the En Bas Saline Site, Haiti." In *Columbus and His World*, edited by Donald T. Gerace, 341–59. San Salvador Island, Bahamas: College Center of the Finger Lakes Bahamian Field Station.
DeBoer, Warren R.
    1975. "The Archeological Evidence for Manioc Cultivation: A Cautionary Note." *American Antiquity* 40(1): 419–32.
Denevan, William M., ed.
    1976. *Native Population of the Americas in 1492.* Madison: University of Wisconsin Press.
Didiez Burgos, Ramón J.
    1974. *Guanahani y Mayaguan.* Santo Domingo: Sociedad Dominicana de Geografía.
Dobyns, Henry F.
    1976. *Native American Historical Demography.* Bloomington: University of Indiana Press.
    1983. *Their Number Become Thinned: Native American Population Dynamics in Eastern North America.* Knoxville: University of Tennessee Press.
Drennan, R. D., and C. A. Uribe, eds.
    1987. *Chiefdoms in the Americas.* Landon, Md.: University Press of America.
Dreyfus, Simone
    1981. "Notes sur la Chefferie Taino d'Aiti: Capacitée productrices, ressources alimentaires, pouvoirs dan une société précolombienne de forêt tropicale." *Société des Americanistes.*
Dreyfus-Gamelon, Simone
    1976. "Remarques sur l'organisation socio-politique des Caraïbes insulaires du XVIIème siècle." *Proceedings of the Sixth International Congress for the Study of the Pre-Columbian Cultures of the Lesser Antilles,* 87–97.

Earle, Timothy K.
1977. "A Reappraisal of Redistribution: Complex Hawaiian Chiefdoms," In *Exchange Systems in Prehistory*, edited by Timothy K. Earle, 213–29. New York: Academic Press.
1987. "Chiefdoms in Archaeological and Ethnohistorical Perspective." *Annual Review of Anthropology* 16:279–308.
Ekholm, Gordon
1946. "The Probable Uses of Mexican Stone Yokes." *American Anthropologist* 48(4): 53–56.
1961. "Puerto Rican Stone Collars as Ballgame Belts." In *Essays in Pre-Columbian Art and Archaeology*, edited by S. K. Lothrop et al. Cambridge: Harvard University Press.
Febvre, Lucien, and H. J. Martin
1971. *L'apparation du livre*. Paris: Institute Academique.
Feinman, G., and J. Neitzel
1984. "Too Many Types: An Overview of Sedentary Prestate Societies in the Americas." *Advances in Archaeological Method and Theory* 7:39–102.
Fewkes, J. W.
1970 [1907]. *The Aborigines of Porto Rico*. New York: Johnson Reprint. Originally "The Aborigines of Porto Rico and Neighboring Islands." *Bureau of American Ethnology Annual Report* 25: 1–220.
Flannery, Kent V.
1975. "La evolución cultural de la civilizaciones." *Cuadernos Anagrama* no. 103.
Floyd, Troy S.
1973. *The Columbus Dynasty in the Caribbean, 1492–1526*. Albuquerque: University of New Mexico Press.
Fox, Gustavus V.
1880. "An Attempt to Solve the Problem of the First Landing Place of Columbus in the New World." *Report to the Superintendent of the U.S. Coast and Geodetic Survey*. Washington, D.C.: Government Printing Office.
Frati, S.
1929. *El mapa más antigua de la Isla de Santo Domingo—1516 y Pedro Martir de Anglería*. Santo Domingo: Gobierno Dominicano.
Fried, Morton
1967. *The Evolution of Political Society*. New York: Random House.
Friede, Juan
1971. "Las Casas and Indigenism is the Sixteenth Century." In *Bartolomé de las Casas in History*, edited by Juan Friede and Benjamin Keen, 127–236. DeKalb: Northern Illinois University Press.

Friede, Juan, and Benjamin Keen, eds.
   1971. *Bartolomé de las Casas in History*. DeKalb: Northern Illinois University Press.
Friedman, Jonathan
   1974. "Tribes, States, and Transformations." In *Marxist Analyses in Social Anthropology*, edited by Maurice Bloch, 161–202. London: Malaby Press.
   1982. "Catastrophe and Continuity in Social Evolution." In *Theory and Explanation in Archaeology*, edited by C. Renfrew, M. J. Rowlands, and B. A. Segraves. New York: Academic Press.
Fuente García, Santiago de la
   1976. *Geografía dominicana*. Santo Domingo: Editorial Colegial Quisqueyana.
Fuson, Robert H.
   1985. "The Diario de Colón: A Legacy of Poor Transcription, Translation, and Interpretation." In *In the Wake of Columbus*, edited by Louis De Vorsey II and John Parker, 51–76. Detroit: Wayne University Press.
García Arévalo, Manuel
   1977. *El arte taíno de la República Dominicana*. Barcelona: Museo del Hombre Dominicano.
   1983. "El murciélago en la mitología y el arte taíno." In *La cultura taína*, 109–17. Madrid: Comisión Nacional para la Celebración del V Centenario del Descubrimiento de América, 109–17.
García Goyco, Osvaldo
   1984. *Influencias mayas y aztecas en los Taínos*. San Juan, P.R.: Ediciones Xibalbay.
Geertz, Clifford
   1973. *The Interpretation of Cultures*. New York: Basic Books.
   1980. *Negara: The Theatre State in Nineteenth-Century Bali*. Princeton: Princeton University Press.
Gerace, D. T., ed.
   1987. *Proceedings of the First San Salvador Conference: Columbus and His World*. Fort Lauderdale, Fla.: CCFL Bahamian Field Station.
Giménez Fernández, Manuel
   1951. "El alzamiento de Fernando Cortés según las cuentas de la Casa de la Contratación." *Revista de Historia de América* 31:1–58.
   1971. "Fray Bartolomé de Las Casas: A Biographical Sketch." In *Bartolomé de Las Casas*, edited by Juan Friede and Benjamin Keen, 67–126. DeKalb: Northern Illinois University Press.
Gomara, Lopez de
   1932. *Historia general de las Indias*. 2 vols. Madrid: Espasa-Salpe.
Gómez Acevedo, Labor, and Manuel Ballesteros Gaibrois
   1980. *Vida y cultura precolombinas de Puerto Rico*. Río Piedras, P.R.: Editorial Cultural.

Goodwin, R. Christopher
 1978. "The Lesser Antillean Archaic: New Data from St. Kitts." *Journal of the Virgin Islands Archaeological Society* 5:6–16.
 1979. "The Prehistoric Cultural Ecology of St. Kitts, West Indies: A Case Study in Island Archaeology." Ph.D. diss. (University Microfilms 8009711), Arizona State University.
 1980. "Demographic Changes and the Crab-Shell Dichotomy." *Proceedings of the Eighth International Congress for the Study of Pre-Columbian Cultures of the Lesser Antilles*, 45–68.
Goodwin, R. Christopher, and Jeffery B. Walker
 1975. *Villa taína de Boquerón*. San Juan, P.R.: Interamerican University Press.
Haas, Jonathan
 1982. *The Evolution of the Prehistoric State*. New York: Columbia University Press.
Hanke, Lewis
 1951. "Estudio preliminar." In *Historia de las Indias*, by Bartolomé de Las Casas, x–lxxxvi. Mexico City: Fondo de Cultura Económica.
 1970. "The Relevance of Bartolomé de Las Casas to Our Contemporary World." In *Tears of the Indians*, by Bartolomé de Las Casas, i–xvii. Williamstown, Mass.: John Lilburne.
Harrington, M. R.
 1921. *Cuba before Columbus*. 2 vols. New York: Museum of the American Indian, Heye Foundation.
Harris, Marvin
 1979. *Cultural Materialism*. New York: Random House.
 1982. *El materialismo cultural*. Madrid: Alianza Universidad.
Helms, Mary
 1979. *Ancient Panama: Chiefs in Search of Power*. Austin: University of Texas Press.
 1980. "Succession to High Office in Pre-Columbian Circum-Caribbean Chiefdoms." *Man* 15:718–31.
 1988. *Ulysses' Sail: An Ethnographic Odyssey of Power, Knowledge, and Geographical Distance*. Princeton: Princeton University Press.
Henige, David
 1978a. "On the Contact Population of Hispaniola: History as Higher Mathematics." *Hispanic American Historical Review* 58(2): 217–37.
 1978b. "David Henige's Reply." *Hispanic American Historical Review* 58(4): 709–12. (reply to Zambardino 1978)
Herrera, Antonio de
 1975. *Historia de la Conquista de la Isla Española*. Edited by Pedro J. Santiago. Santo Domingo: Publicaciones del Museo de las Cases Reales.

Herrera Fritot, René
1936. *Culturas aborígines de las Antillas.* Havana: Lyceum.
Hodder, Ian
1987a. "The Contextual Analysis of Symbolic Meanings." In *The Archaeology of Contextual Meanings,* edited by Ian Hodder, 1–10. Cambridge: Cambridge University Press.
Hodder, Ian, ed.
1987b. *Archaeology as Long-Term History.* Cambridge: Cambridge University Press.
Hoffman, Charles A., Jr.
1963. "Archaeological Investigations on Antigua, West Indies." Master's thesis, University of Florida, Gainesville.
1979. "The Ceramic Typology of the Mill Reef Site, Antigua, Leeward Islands." *Journal of the Virgin Islands Archaeological Society* 7:35–51.
1987. "Archaeological Investigations at the Long Bay Site, San Salvador, Bahamas." In *Proceedings of the First San Salvador Conference: Columbus and His World,* edited by D. T. Gerace, 237–45. Fort Lauderdale, Fla.: CCFL Bahamian Field Station.
Irving, Washington
1828. *A History of the Life and Voyages of Christopher Columbus.* 3 vols. New York: G. and C. Carvill.
Jane, Cecil
1930. *The Voyage of Christopher Columbus.* London: Argonaut Press.
Judge, Joseph
1986. "Where Columbus Found the New World." *National Geographic Magazine* 170(5): 566–99.
Keegan, William F.
1984. "Columbus and the City of Gold." *Journal of the Bahamas Historical Society* 6:34–39.
1985. "Dynamic Horticulturalists: Population Expansion in the Prehistoric Bahamas." Ph.D. diss., University of California, Los Angeles.
1986. "The Ecology of Lucayan Fishing Practices." *American Antiquity* 51(4): 816–25.
1987. "Diffusion of Maize from South America: The Antillean Connection Reconsidered." In *Emergent Horticultural Economies of the Eastern Woodlands,* edited by William F. Keegan, 329–44. Carbondale: Southern Illinois University Center for Archaeological Investigations, Occasional Paper 7.
1988. "Transition from a Terrestrial to a Maritime Economy: The Isotopic Record." Paper presented at the fifty-third annual meeting of the Society for American Archaeology, Phoenix, Arizona, April 27–May 1.
Keegan, William F., and M. J. DeNiro
1988. "Stable Carbon and Nitrogen Isotope Ratios Used to Study Coral

Reef and Terrestrial Components of Prehistoric Bahamian Diet." *American Antiquity* 53(2):320–36.

Keegan, William F., and J. M. Diamond

1987. "Colonization of Islands by Humans: A Biogeographical Perspective." *Advances in Archaeological Method and Theory* 10:49–92.

Keegan, William F., and Morgan D. Maclachlan

1989. "The Evolution of Avunculocal Chiefdoms: A Reconstruction of Taíno Kinship and Politics." *American Anthropologist* 91(3):613–30.

Kerr, Robert

1824. *General History and Collection of Voyages and Travels, Arranged in Systematic Order, Forming a Complete History of the Origin and Progress of Navigation, Discovery, and Commerce, by Sea and Land, from the Earliest Ages to the Present Time.* Vol. 3. Edinburgh: William Blackwood.

Kirch, Patrick V.

1984. *The Evolution of the Polynesian Chiefdoms.* Cambridge: Cambridge University Press.

Koslowski, Janusz K.

1978. "In Search of the Evolution Pattern of the Preceramic Cultures of the Caribbean." *Boletín del Museo del Hombre Dominicano* 13:61–79.

Krieger, Herbert W.

1930. "The Aborigines of the Ancient Island of Hispaniola." *Annual Report of the Smithsonian Institution for 1929*, 473–506.

1931. *Aboriginal Indian Pottery of the Dominican Republic.* Washington, D.C.: United States National Museum, Bulletin 156, Smithsonian Institution.

Lamb, Ursula

1956. *Frey Nicolás de Ovando, Governador de Indias (1501–1509).* Madrid: Consejo Superior de Investigaciónes Científicas.

Las Casas, Fray Bartolomé de

1951. *Historia de las Indias.* 3 vols. Mexico City: Fondo de Cultura Económica.

1966. *Brevísima relación de la destrucción de las Indias.* Buenos Aires: Universidad de Buenos Aires.

1967. *Apologética historia sumaria.* 3 vols. Mexico City: Universidad Nacional Autónoma de México, Instituto de Investigaciones Históricas.

Lathrap, Donald

1970. *The Upper Amazon.* New York: Praeger.

Lemle, M.

1971. *The Tupi-Guaranían Family.* Tupi Studies, part 1. Dallas: Summer Institute of Linguistic Publications in Linguistics, 39.

LeRoy Ladurie, Emmanuel
  1981. *The Mind and Method of the Historian.* Translated by Siân Reynolds and Ben Reynolds. Chicago: University of Chicago Press.
Link, Edwin A., and Marion C. Link
  1958. *A New Theory on Columbus's Voyage through the Bahamas.* Washington, D.C.: Smithsonian Miscellaneous Collections, no. 135.
López-Baralt, Mercedes
  1976. *El mito taíno: Raíz y proyecciones en la Amazonia continental.* Buenos Aires: Ediciones Huracán.
Loven, Sven
  1935. *The Origins of Tainan Culture, West Indies.* Göteborg: Elanders Bokfryekeri Akfiebolag.
Lundberg, Emily R.
  1980. "Old and New Problems in the Study of Antillean Aceramic Traditions." *Proceedings of the Eighth International Congress for the Study of Pre-Columbian Cultures of the Lesser Antilles,* 131–38.
McElroy, John W.
  1941. "The Ocean Navigation of Columbus on His First Voayge." *American Neptune* 1:209–40.
McGovern, Thomas H.
  1980. "Cows, Harp Seals, and Churchbells: Adaptation and Extinction in Norse Greenland." *Human Ecology* 8(3): 245–75.
McKusick, Marshall
  1960. "The Distribution of Ceramic Styles in the Lesser Antilles." Ph.D. diss., Yale University.
MacNutt, Francis Augustus
  1970. "Introduction." In *De Orbe Novo: The Eight Decades of Peter Martyr D'Anghera,* by Peter Martyr D'Anghera, 1–48. New York: Burt Franklin.
Major, R. H.
  1924. *Four Voyages to the New World.* Magnolia, Mass.: Peter Smith.
Mandeville, Sir John
  1983. *The Travels of Sir John Mandeville.* London: Penguin Books.
Marco Polo
  1908. *The Travels of Marco Polo the Venetian.* London: J. M. Dent and Sons.
Markham, Clements R.
  1893. "Introduction." In *The Journal of Christopher Columbus (during His First Voyage, 1492–1493), and Documents Relating to the Voyages of John Cabot and Gaspar Corte Real,* by Christopher Columbus. London: Hakluyt Society.
Martyr D'Anghera, Peter
  1970. *De Orbe Novo: The Eight Decades of Peter Martyr D'Anghera.* Translated by Francis Augustus MacNutt. New York: Burt Franklin.

Meggers, Betty J.
    1971. *Amazonia: Man and Culture in a Counterfeit Paradise.* Chicago: Aldine.
Meggers, Betty J., and Clifford Evans
    1961. "An Experimental Formulation of Horizon Styles in the Tropical Forest Area of South America." In *Essays in Pre-Columbian Art and Archaeology*, edited by S. K. Lothrop et al., 46–82. Cambridge: Harvard University Press.
Molander, Arne B.
    1981. "Columbus Landed Here—or Did He?," *Américas*, vol. 33.
Montlezun, Baron de
    1828. "Revue nautique du premier voyage de Christophe Colomb." *Nouvelles Annales des Voyages et Sciences Geographiques* 10:299–350.
Morbán Laucer, Fernando
    1979. *Ritos funerarios: Acción del fuego y medio ambiente en las osamentas precolombinas.* Santo Domingo: Academia de Ciencias de La República Dominicana.
Morison, Samuel
    1942. *Admiral of the Ocean Sea.* Boston: Little, Brown.
Morison, Samuel Eliot, and Mauricio Obregón
    1964. *The Caribbean As Columbus Saw It.* Boston: Little, Brown.
Moscoso, Francisco
    1978. "Tributo y formación de clases en la sociedad de los Taínos de las Antillas," *Proceedings of the Seventh International Congress for the Study of Pre-Columbian Cultures of the Lesser Antilles*, 305–23.
    1983. "Parentesco y clase en los cacicazgos taínos: El caso de los naborias." *Proceedings of the Ninth International Congress for the Study of Pre-Columbian Cultures of the Lesser Antilles*, 485–94.
Moya Pons, Frank
    1983. *Manual de historia dominicana.* 7th ed. Santiago, Dominican Republic: Universidad Católica Madre y Maestra.
Murdock, J. B.
    1884. "The Cruise of Columbus in the Bahamas, 1492." *Proceedings of the U.S. Naval Institute*, April, 449–86.
Nau, Emile
    1894. *Histoire des caciques d'Haití.* Paris. Also published as *Historia de los caciques de Haití*, by Emilie Nau. Santo Domingo: Sociedad Dominicana de Bibliófilos (1983).
Navarrete, Martin Fernández, ed.
    1825–37. *Collección de los viages y descubrimientos que hicieron por mar los Españoles desde fines del siglo XV.* Five vols. Madrid.
Nicholson, Desmond V.
    1976a. "An Antigua Shell Midden with Ceramic and Archaic Compo-

nents." *Proceedings of the Sixth International Congress for the Study of Pre-Columbian Cultures of the Lesser Antilles,* 258–63.

1976b. "Artifact Types of Preceramic Antigua," *Proceedings of the Sixth International Congress for the Study of Pre-Columbian Cultures of the Lesser Antilles,* 246–58.

1976c. "Pre-Columbian Seafaring Capabilities in the Lesser Antilles." *Proceedings of the Sixth International Congress for the Study of Pre-Columbian Cultures of the Lesser Antilles,* 98–105.

1983. *The Story of the Arawaks in Antigua and Barbuda.* Antigua: Antigua Archaeological Society.

Noble, G. K.
1965. "Proto-Arawaken and Its Descendants." *International Journal of American Linguistics* 31(3): 2–22.

O'Gorman, Edmundo
1967. "La Apologética Historia, su génesis y elaboración, su estructura y su sentido." In *Apologética historia sumaria,* by Bartolomé de las Casas. Mexico City: Universidad Nacional Antónoma de México, Instituto de Investigaciónes Históricas.

Olsen, Fred
1974a. "The Arawak Ball Court at Antigua and the Prototype Zemi." *Proceedings of the Fifth International Congress for the Study of Pre-Columbian Cultures of the Lesser Antilles,* 11–12.

1974b. *On the Trail of the Arawaks.* Norman: University of Oklahoma Press.

Ortega, Elpidio
1978. "Informe sobre investigaciones arqueológicas realizadas in la región este del país, zona costera desde Macao a Punta Espada." *Boletín del Museo del Hombre Dominicano* 11:77–99.

Oviedo y Valdés, Gonzalo Fernández
1959. *Historia general y natural de las Indias.* 5 vols. Biblioteca de Autores Españoles, vols. 117–21. Madrid: Gráficas Orbe.

Pané, Ramón
1974. *Relación acerca de las antigüedades de los Indios.* Mexico City: Universidad de México.

Pantel, Agamemnón Gus
1983. "Orígenes y definición de la cultura taína: Sus antecedentes tecnológicos en el precerámico." In *La cultura taína,* 9–13. Madrid: Comisión Nacional para la Celebración del V Centenario del Descubrimiento de América.

Parker, John
1985. "The Columbus Landfall Problem: A Historical Perspective." In *In the Wake of Columbus: Islands and Controversy,* edited by Louis De Vorsey, Jr., and John Parker, 1–28. Detroit: Wayne State University Press.

Perez, Alejandro Raymundo
1987. *The Columbus Landfall in America and the Hidden Clues in His Journal.* Washington, D.C.: Abbe Publishers Association.
Pérez de Tudela Bueso, Juan
1954. "La negociación colombina de las Indias." *Revista de Indias* 15(59): 11–88.
1955. "Política de poblamiento y política de contratación de las Indias (1502–1505)." *Revista des Indias* 15(61–62):371–420.
1983. *Mirabilis in Alta: Estudio crítico sobre el origen y significado del proyecto descubridor de Cristóbal Colón.* Madrid: Consejo Superior de Investigaciones Científicas, Instituto Gonzales Fernández de Oviedo.
Pichardo Moya, Felipe
1956. *Los Aborígines de las Antillas.* Mexico: Fondo de Cultura Económica.
Pike, Ruth
1966. *Enterprise and Adventure: The Genoese in Seville and the Opening of the New World.* Ithaca: Cornell University Press.
1972. *Aristocrats and Traders: Sevillian Society in the Sixteenth Century.* Ithaca: Cornell University Press.
Raccolta di Documenti e Studi
1893. *Raccolta di documenti e studi.* Rome: R. Commissione Colombiana, Pel Quarto Centenario Dalla Scoperta Dell'America.
Ramenofsky, Ann F.
1987. *Vectors of Death: The Archaeology of European Contact.* Albuquerque: University of New Mexico Press.
Ramos Pérez, Demetrio
1982. *El conflicto de las Lanzas Jinetas.* Santo Domingo: Fundación García Arévalo.
Remeu de Armas, Antonio
1985. *Nueva luz sobre las Capitulaciones de Santa Fe de 1492 concertadas entre los reyes católicos y Cristóbal Colón: Estudio institucional y diplomático.* Madrid: Consejo Superior de Investigaciones Científicas.
Rodríguez Demorizi, Emilio
1971. *Los Dominicos y las encomiendas de Indios de la Isla Española.* Santo Domingo: Academia Dominicana de la Historia, vol. 30.
Roosevelt, Anna C.
1980. *Parmana: Prehistoric Maize and Manioc Subsistence along the Amazon and Orinoco.* New York: Academic Press.
Rosenblat, Angel
1967. *La población de América en 1492: Viejos y nuevos cáculos.* México: El Colegio de México.
1976. "The Population of Hispaniola at the Time of Columbus." In *The Native Population of the Americas in 1492*, edited by W. M. Denevan, 43–66. Madison: University of Wisconsin Press.

Roth, H. Ling
1887. "The Aborigines of Hispaniola." *Journal of the Anthropological Institute of Great Britain and Ireland* 16:247–86.
Rouse, Irving
N.d. "Ancestries of the Tainos: Amazonian or Circum-Caribbean." Unpublished manuscript.
1939. *Prehistory in Haiti, a Study in Method*. New Haven: Yale University Publications in Anthropology, no. 21.
1941. *Culture of the Ft. Liberté Region, Haiti*. New Haven: Yale University Publications in Anthropology, no. 24.
1942. *Archaeology of the Maniabon Hills, Cuba*. New Haven: Yale University Publications in Anthropology, no. 26.
1948. "The West Indies: An Introduction; The Ciboney; The Arawak; The Carib." In *Handbook of South American Indians*, edited by Julian Steward, 495–565. Washington, D.C.: Bureau of American Ethnology Bulletin.
1951. "Areas and Periods of Culture in the Greater Antilles." *Southwestern Journal of Anthropology* 7(3): 248–65.
1958. "The Inference of Migrations from Anthropological Evidence." In *Migrations in New World Culture History*, edited by R. H. Thompson, 63–68. University of Arizona Press, Social Science Bulletin 27(2).
1964. "Prehistory of the West Indies." *Science* 144(3618): 369–75.
1966. "Mesoamerica and the Eastern Caribbean Area." *Handbook of Mesoamerican Indians* 4:234–42.
1974. "Cultural Development on Antigua, West Indies: A Progress Report," Paper presented at the Forty-first International Congress of Americanists, Mexico City.
1976. "The Saladoid Sequence on Antigua and Its Aftermath." *Proceedings of the Sixth International Congress for the Study of Pre-Columbian Cultures of the Lesser Antilles*, 35–41.
1982. "Ceramic and Religious Development in the Greater Antilles." *Journal of New World Archaeology* 5(2): 45–55.
1985. "Arawakan Phylogeny, Caribbean Chronology, and Their Implications for the Study of Population Movement." In *La esfera de interacción de la cuenca del Orinoco: Festschrift a Marshall Durbin*. Caracas: Instituto Venezolano de Investigaciones Científicas.
1986. *Migrations in Prehistory*. New Haven: Yale University Press.
Rouse, Irving, and Ricardo E. Alegría
1989. *Excavations at María de la Cruz and Hacienda Grande, Loiza, Puerto Rico*. New Haven: Yale University Publications in Anthropology.
Rouse, Irving, and Louis Allaire
1978. "Caribbean Chronology." In *Chronologies in New World Archaeology*, 431–81. New York: Academic Press.

Rouse, Irving, and José M. Cruxent
  1963. *Venezuelan Archaeology.* New Haven: Yale University Press.
Rouse, Irving, and Clark Moore
  1983. "Cultural Sequence in Southwestern Haiti." *Proceedings of the Ninth International Congress for the Study of Pre-Columbian Cultures of the Lesser Antilles,* 1–17.
Sahlins, Marshall
  1976. *Culture and Practical Reason.* Chicago: University of Chicago Press.
  1981. *Historical Metaphor and Mythical Reality: Structure in the Early History of the Sandwich Islands Kingdom.* Ann Arbor: University of Michigan Press.
  1985. *Islands of History.* Chicago: University of Chicago Press.
Sanders, William T., and Barbara J. Price
  1968. *Mesoamerica: The Evolution of a Civilization.* New York: Random House.
Sanoja Obediente, Mario
  1983. "El origen de la sociedad taína y el formativo suramericano." In *La cultura taína,* 37–47. Madrid: Comisión Nacional para la Celebración del V Centenario del Descubrimiento de América.
Sanoja Obediente, Mario, and Iraida Vargas
  1983. "New Light on the Prehistory of Eastern Venezuela." In *Advances in New World Archaeology,* no. 2, edited by F. Wendorf and A. E. Close, 205–43. New York: Academic Press.
Sauer, Carl O.
  1966. *The Early Spanish Main.* Berkeley: University of California Press.
Sears, William H.
  1977. "Seaborn Contacts between Early Cultures in Lower Southeastern United States and Middle through South America." In *The Sea in the Pre-Columbian World,* edited by E. P. Benson, 1–13. Washington, D.C.: Dumbarton Oaks.
  1982. *Fort Center: An Archaeological Site on the Lake Okeechobee Basin.* Gainesville: University Presses of Florida.
Sears, William H., and S. D. Sullivan
  1978. "Bahamas Prehistory." *American Anthropologist* 43:3–25.
Service, Elman R.
  1971. *Primitive Social Organization.* 2d ed. New York: Random House.
Siegel, Peter E.
  1988. "Site Structure, Demography, and Social Complexity in the Early Ceramic-Age of the Caribbean." Paper presented at the fifty-third annual meeting of the Society for American Archaeology, April 27–May 1, Phoenix, Arizona.

Siegel, Peter E., and David J. Bernstein
  1987. "Sampling for Site Structure and Spatial Organization in the Saladoid: A Case Study." Paper presented at the Twelfth International Congress for Caribbean Archaeology, Cayenne, French Guiana.
Sleight, Frederick W.
  1962. "Archaeological Reconnaissance of the Island of St. John, United
  States Virgin Islands." William L. Bryant Foundation American Studies,
  no 3. Gainesville, Fla.
  1965. "Certain Environmental Considerations in West Indian Archaeology." American Antiquity 31:226–31.
Spencer, C. S.
  1987. "Rethinking the Chiefdom." In Chiefdoms in the Americas, edited
  by R. D. Drennan and C. A. Uribe, 369–90. Landon, Md.: University
  Press of America.
Spores, Ronald
  1980. "New World Ethnohistory and Archaeology, 1970–1980." Annual
  Review of Anthropology 9:575–603.
Stone, Lawrence
  1979. "The Revival of Narrative: Reflections on a New Old History."
  Past and Present 85:3–24.
Sturtevant, William C.
  1960. The Significance of Ethnological Similarities between Southeastern
  North America and the Antilles. New Haven: Yale University Publications in Anthroplogy, no. 64.
  1961. "Taino Agriculture." In The Evolution of Horticultural Systems in
  Native South America: Causes and Consequences, 69–82. Caracas: Sociedad de Ciencias Naturales.
Sued Badillo, Jalil
  1978. Los Caribes: Realidad o Fábula. Río Piedras, P.R.: Editorial Antillana.
  1979. La mujer indigena y su sociedad 2d ed. Río Piedras, P.R.: Editoral
  Antillana.
  1983. Cristóbal Colón y la esclavitud del Indio en las Antillas. San Juan
  P.R.: Fundación Arqueológica, Antropológica, Histórica de Puerto
  Rico.
  1985. "Las cacicas indoantillanas." Revista del Instituto de Cultura Puertorriqueña 87:17–26.
Sullivan, S. D.
  1981. "Prehistoric Patterns of Exploitation and Colonization in the Turks
  and Caicos Islands." Ph.D. diss., University of Illinois, Urbana.
Tabío, Ernesto E., and Estrella Rey
  1966. Prehistoria de Cuba. Havana: Departamento de Antropología,
  Academia de Ciencias de Cuba.

Tavares, Julia
1978. *Cultura y arte precolombino del Caribe.* Santo Domingo: Museo del Hombre Dominicano.
Taylor, Douglas, and B. J. Hoff
1980. "The Linguistic Repertory of the Island Carib in the Seventeenth Century: The Men's Language—a Carib Pidgin." *International Journal of American Linguistics* 46:301–12.
Taylor, Douglas, and Irving Rouse
1955. "Linguistic and Archaeological Time Depth in the West Indies." *International Journal of American Linguistics* 21(2): 379–92.
Thurn, E. F.
1887. "On the Races of the West Indies." *Journal of the Anthropological Institute of Great Britain and Ireland* 16:105–15.
Todorov, Tzvetlan
1984. *The Conquest of America.* New York: Harper and Row.
Tolentino Rojas, Vicente
1944. *Historia de la división territorial, 1492–1943.* Santo Domingo: Ediciones del Gobierno Dominicano.
Upham, S.
1987. "A Theoretical Consideration of Middle Range Societies." In *Chiefdoms in the Americas,* edited by R. D. Drennan and C. A. Uribe. Landon, Md.: University Press of America.
Varnhagen, Francisco Adolfo de
1864. "La verdadera Guahani de Colon." *Annales de la Universidad de Chile* 24:1–20.
Vega, Bernardo
1980. *Los cacicazgos de la Hispaniola.* Santo Domingo: Museo del Hombre Dominicano.
Veloz Maggiolo, Marcio
1972. *Arqueología prehistórica de Santo Domingo.* Singapore: McGraw-Hill Far Eastern Publishers.
1977. *Medioambiente y adaptacion humana en la prehistoria de Santo Domingo.* Vol. 2. Santo Domingo: Universidad Autónoma de Santo Domingo, Colección Historia y Sociedad 30.
1983. "Para una definición de la cultura taína." In *La cultura taína,* 15–21. Madrid: Comisión Nacional para la Celebración del V Centenario del Descubrimiento de América.
Veloz Maggiolo, Marcio, and Elpidio Ortega
1973. "El precerámico de Santo Domingo, nuevos lugares, y su posible relación con otros puntos del área Antillana." *Museo del Hombre Dominicano, Papeles Ocasionales,* no. 1.
1980. "Nuevos hallazgos arqueológicos en la costa norte de Santo Domingo." *Boletín del Museo del Hombre Dominicano* 13:11–48.

Veloz Maggiolo, Marcio, Elpidio Ortega, and Angel Caba Fuentes
  1981. *Los modos de vida Mellacoides y sus posibles origenes: Un estudio interpretativo.* Santo Domingo: Museo del Hombre Dominicano.
Veloz Maggiolo, Marcio, Elpidio Ortega, and Plinio Pina Peña
  1973. "Fechas de radio carbón para el período ceramista en la República Dominicana." *Boletín del Museo del Hombre Dominicano* 2:47–56.
Veloz Maggiolo, Marcio, Elpidio Ortega, Plinio Pina Peña, Renato Rimoli, and Fernando Luna Calderón
  1972. "El cemeterio de la 'Union,' provincia de Puerto Plata." *Boletín del Museo del Hombre Dominicano* 2:130–55.
Veloz Maggiolo, Marcio, R. O. Rimoli, F. L. Calderón, and J. E. Nadal
  1977. *Arqueología de Punta de Garza.* San Pedro de Macoris, Dominican Republic: Universidad Central del Este.
Veloz Maggiolo, Marcio, I. Vargas, M. Sanoja Obediente, and F. Luna Calderón
  1976. *Arqueología de Yuma (República Dominicana).* Santo Domingo: Taller.
Veloz Maggiolo, Marcio, and Bernardo Vega
  1982. "The Antillean Preceramic: A New Approximation." *Journal of New World Archaeology* 5(1): 33–44.
Verhoog, Pieter
  1947. *Guanahaní Again.* Amsterdam.
  1985. "Columbus Landed on Caicos." In *In the Wake of Columbus*, edited by Louis De Vorsey, Jr., and John Parker. Detroit: Wayne State University Press.
Versteeg, Aad
  1980. "Prehistoric Cultural Ecology of the Coastal Plain of Western Surinam." *Proceedings of the Eighth International Congress for the Study of Pre-Columbian Cultures of the Lesser Antilles*, 88–97.
  1987a. "Archaeological Research on St. Eustatius: Indian Farmers in the Netherlands Antilles in the Fifth Century A.D." *Netherlands Foundation for the Advancement of Tropical Research, Report for the Year 1986*, 25–40.
  1987b. "Saladoid Houses and Functional Areas around Them: The Golden Rock Site on St. Eustatius (Netherlands Antilles)." Paper presented at the Twelfth Meeting of the International Association for Caribbean Archaeology, Cayenne, French Guiana.
Vignaud, Henry
  1902. *Toscanelli and Columbus.* New York: E. P. Dutton.
Watters, David R.
  1980. "Transect Surveying and Prehistoric Site Locations on Barbuda and Montserrat, Leeward Islands, West Indies." Ph.D. diss., University of Pittsburgh.

Wilson, Samuel M.

1985a. "The Spanish Caciques: Renegades in the Chiefdoms of the Caribbean." Paper presented at the annual meeting of the American Society for Ethnohistory.

1985b. "Taíno Elite Integration and Societal Complexity on Hispaniola." Paper presented at the Eleventh International Congress for Caribbean Archaeology, San Juan, Puerto Rico, June 28–July 3.

1986. "The Conquest of the Caribbean Chiefdoms: Sociopolitical Change on Prehispanic Hispaniola." Ph.D. diss., University of Chicago.

1989. "The Prehistoric Settlement Pattern of Nevis, West Indies." *Journal of Field Archaeology* 16(4):427–50.

Wing, Elizabeth S., and S. Scudder

1980. "Use of Animals by the Prehistoric Inhabitants on St. Kitts, West Indies." *Proceedings of the Eighth International Congress for the Study of Pre-Columbian Cultures of the Lesser Antilles*, 237–45.

1983. "Animal Exploitation by Prehistoric Peoples Living on a Tropical Marine Edge." In *Animals and Archaeology*, vol. 2: *Shell Middens, Fishes, and Birds*, edited by C. Grigson and J. Clutton-Brock, 197–210. Oxford: B.A.R. International Series 183.

Zabala, Silvio

1949. "Los trabajadores antillanos en el siglo XVI." *Estudios Indianos* 1949:95–204.

Zambardino, R. A.

1978. "Critique of David Henige's 'On the Contact Population of Hispaniola: History as Higher Mathematics.'" *Hispanic American Historical Review* 58(4): 700–708.

Zucchi, Alberta, Kay Tarble, and Eduardo Vaz

1984. "The Ceramic Sequence and New TL and C-14 Dates for the Aguerito Site on the Middle Orinoco, Venezuela." *Journal of Field Archaeology* 11:155–80.

Index

165